W9-BDS-806

Differentiating Instruction in a Whole-Group Setting

Differentiating Instruction in a Whole-Group Setting

Taking the Easy First Steps into Differentiation, Grades 7–12

BY BETTY HOLLAS

Crystal Springs
BOOKS

A division of SDE Staff Development for EDUCATORS

Peterborough, New Hampshire

Published by Crystal Springs Books
A division of Staff Development for Educators (SDE)
10 Sharon Road
PO Box 500
Peterborough, NH 03458
1-800-321-0401
www.crystalsprings.com
www.sde.com

© 2007 Crystal Springs Books
Published 2007
Printed in the United States of America
11 10 09 08 07 1 2 3 4 5

ISBN: 978-1-884548-96-3

Library of Congress Cataloging-in-Publication Data

Hollas, Betty, 1948-
  Differentiating instruction in a whole-group setting : taking the easy first steps into differentiation,
grades 7-12 / by Betty Hollas.
       p. cm.
  Includes index.
  ISBN 978-1-884548-96-3
  1. Individualized instruction. 2. Middle school teaching. 3. High school teaching. I. Title.

  LB1031.H633 2007
  373.139'4—dc22

                                            2007000964

Editor: Sharon Smith
Art director, designer, and production coordinator: Soosen Dunholter
Illustrator: Marci McAdam

Crystal Springs Books grants teachers the right to photocopy the reproducibles from this book for
classroom use. No other part of this book may be reproduced in whole or in part, or stored in a
retrieval system, or transmitted in any form or by any means, electronic, mechanical, photocopying,
recording, or otherwise, without permission of the publisher.

For Paul, Lindsay, Jackson, Beth Ann, Rocky, and Blitz

Contents

	TEXT	REPRO
ACKNOWLEDGMENTS	9	
INTRODUCTION	11	
CHAPTER 1: STUDENT ENGAGEMENT WINDOW	14	
Strategy #1: Appointment Calendar	17	102
Strategy #2: Timed-Pair Paraphrase	19	
Strategy #3: Carousel Your Way Through a K–W–L	20	
Strategy #4: Show—Don't Tell	22	
Strategy #5: That's Me!	23	
Strategy #6: Snowball Fight	24	
Strategy #7: Vote with Your Feet & Not Your Hands	26	
Strategy #8: What's My Name?	27	
Strategy #9: Circle the Category	28	
Strategy #10: Milling to Music	30	
CHAPTER 2: QUESTIONING WINDOW	33	
Strategy #1: The Parking Lot & Geometric Questions	37	103
Strategy #2: Differentiated Wait Time	38	
Strategy #3: I Do Have a Question	40	105
Strategy #4: Question Stems & Cubing	41	107
Strategy #5: Cubing & Bloom's	44	111
Strategy #6: I Have/Who Has?	46	114
Strategy #7: Question-Tac-Toe	48	115
Strategy #8: Question-Answer Relationships	49	119
Strategy #9: D.E.A.Q.	52	105
Strategy #10: T.H.I.N.K.	53	124
Strategy #11: Talk with F.R.E.D.	54	128
Strategy #12: Planning Questions Are the Key	56	
Strategy #13: Five Questions to Ask	58	129

	TEXT	REPRO

CHAPTER 3: FLEXIBLE GROUPING WINDOW ....60........130

Strategy #1: Fair & Equal Are Not the Same ....66...........132

Strategy #2: Brainstorming A–Z ....67...........133

Strategy #3: Jigsaw 68

Strategy #4: Numbered Heads Together....................70

Strategy #5: Discussion Roles for a Lecture or Video ...71...........134

Strategy #6: Role Cards for Expository Text ....73...........135

Strategy #7: Discussion Cards for Narrative Text ......74...........138

Strategy #8: Think-Tac-Toe ....76...........139

Strategy #9: 4–6–8 ....77...........143

Strategy #10: R.A.F.T. 78

CHAPTER 4: ONGOING ASSESSMENT WINDOW ....81...........144

Strategy #1: Human Continuum 85

Strategy #2: Five-Finger Reading Gauge 86

Strategy #3: Handshake or High Five......................87

Strategy #4: Word Toss 88

Strategy #5: Anticipation Guide 89

Strategy #6: Signal Cards ....90...........147

Strategy #7: Exit Cards 91

Strategy #8: Student Self-Assessment ....92...........148

Strategy #9: Three Facts & a Fib 93

Strategy #10: Learning Logs & Response Journals......94

Strategy #11: Four Square Products ....95...........149

Strategy #12: Kinesthetic Assessment ....96...........150

Strategy #13: Synectics 97

Strategy #14: The Tournament..............................98...........151

CHAPTER 5: GETTING STARTED 100

REPRODUCIBLES 101

RECOMMENDED RESOURCES 153

Print Resources..154

Web Sites 155

INDEX 156

Acknowledgments

Thank you to:

Paul Bonnell, Jill Hollas, Kelli Howe, Jill Lawler, Elizabeth Mordaszweski, Ronnie Nixon, Joni Smith, and Carol Sneed for their indispensable feedback during the writing of this book and for the wonderful suggestions they made, based on their own experiences from many years of teaching at this level.

Soosen Dunholter, designer, art director, and production coordinator, who manages to combine clarity and creativity throughout these pages.

Sharon Smith, who edited this book, and Lorraine Walker, Staff Development for Educators Vice President of Publishing and New Product Development, who had the idea for it.

Deb Fredericks, Publishing Coordinator at Staff Development for Educators, for pulling all the pieces of the publishing process together.

Jim Grant, Executive Director of Staff Development for Educators, speaker, author, and friend; and Char Forsten, Associate Executive Director of Staff Development for Educators, speaker, author, and friend—both of whom continue to be endless sources of ideas, inspiration, and good times.

Introduction

Does the title of this book sound a little strange to you? I think the official word for it would be "oxymoron." How could you possibly differentiate instruction in a whole-group setting? You're probably thinking that this author must be nuts! Actually, I often *am* nuts, as well as sort of wild and crazy. But this time, I really do want to give you something to think about.

Do you know the story about the well-known educator who was talking with the prominent neurosurgeon? The educator said that the decisions teachers make are more important and more difficult than the deci-

sions made in any other profession. The story goes that the neurosurgeon wasn't so sure about that. "How can you say that the decisions a teacher makes are more important and more difficult than decisions made in any other profession?" he wanted to know. "Look at me. I operate on the brain. I've got life and death right there on the table in front of me."

The famous educator responded, "Yes, sir, but you operate on one patient at a time, and that patient is anesthetized!"

In today's classes, your job might be easier if you were like the neurosurgeon and could deal with one "patient" at a time. But we're talking about real life. It's much more likely that you teach students who learn at different rates, who have a wide range of abilities and experiences, and who challenge you at every step of the way. Am I right? It's probably becoming more and more difficult for you to meet the needs of all of your students. It's certainly becoming more and more important. If you're going to meet your state's standards for the wide range of students in your classroom, you're going to need to find ways to adapt your instruction to meet the individual needs of each student.

Does that sound pretty overwhelming? Does it conjure up visions of an individual lesson plan for every student, class periods filled with small groups that are constantly changing, and lots of stations set up in the classroom? Does it also conjure up images of you staying up all night, trying to figure out how to make it all happen?

I'm sure that you want to do a good job and be successful, and I know that you already have plenty of demands on your time. (I have never once had a teacher tell me, "I just wish my administrator would give me more to do during the day!") So this is the point when your instinct might be to throw up your hands and say to yourself, "This, too, shall pass . . . I've been in this business long enough . . . the pendulum swings . . ." and so

STUDENT ENGAGEMENT:
alternatives to the "sit-and-git," "my-way-or-the-highway," "chalk-and-talk," and "spray-and-pray" approaches to whole-group instruction

QUESTIONING:
alternatives to the passive, answer-giving, fact-finding style of whole-group instruction—the one in which the question most often asked is: "Does everyone understand?"

FLEXIBLE GROUPING:
alternatives to the room arrangement preferred by your school's overburdened custodian—the one in which students sit in rows, passively staring at you while fake listening or fake reading for much of the day

ONGOING ASSESSMENT:
alternatives to the teach-teach-teach-then-assess approach to whole-group instruction

on. Then you'd be tempted to shut the door and just continue teaching in the way you're most comfortable—in a whole-group setting.

Relax. You can do that and still differentiate. Really.

You're focusing on the standards and end-of-course objectives your students are expected to meet. You're worrying about how you can possibly address every student's needs and still meet those standards. You have a right to be concerned. But you also need to recognize your own abilities to differentiate instruction in ways that really will help all your students to be successful. And you need to know that you can do this while you're teaching the whole group.

In fact, you may discover that you're already differentiating. You just didn't know it. And you may not have known how much more you could do with differentiation, even within the whole-group setting.

WHAT IS DIFFERENTIATED INSTRUCTION ANYWAY?

In its simplest form, differentiated instruction means that you are consistently and proactively creating different pathways to help all your students to be successful. For example, when you give your students a choice of reading materials related to a common theme, you are differentiating your instruction according to what the students are interested in reading. This is different from having everyone in the class read the same book that you've chosen. It's perhaps *easier* to use just one book, but that's not necessarily the ideal pathway for every student. Make sense? You're probably already thinking of some kind of differentiation you do right now that is proactive and that helps all your students to be successful.

You see, differentiating instruction in a whole-group setting doesn't have to add to the burdens in your classroom. Rather, it can bring fun and excitement to learning, and it can make you a better teacher. You'll be gaining your students' trust by showing them that you genuinely care about them and take a personal interest in each individual. You'll be helping all your students to succeed. That's the goal of differentiation. That's the goal of standards. And I bet that's your goal as a teacher, too.

WINDOWS OF OPPORTUNITY

What differentiated instruction does is to open up more options for more students, so that everybody has a chance to succeed. I like to think of it in terms of windows of opportunity, because that's what differentiated instruction really is—a bunch of opportunities to help every one of your students to succeed. In this book, I'm going to describe four of those windows—student engagement, questioning, flexible grouping, and ongoing assessment—and explain how you can open them for your students.

I'm devoting one chapter to each of these "windows." Each chapter begins with a look at the opportunity itself and then continues with lots of strategies you can use in your classroom. Within each strategy you'll find:

- An overview of the strategy
- The steps or choices involved in using the strategy in your classroom
- A quick look back to see just how this strategy fits into the concept of differentiated instruction

Differentiating instruction in your classroom doesn't have to be overwhelming. It really doesn't. Yes, it adds a certain complexity to teaching. But it's manageable. You can do this. And this book will show you how.

Now, turn the page and say aloud (yes, aloud), "Let's get going!"

Student Engagement Window

In today's middle- and high-school classrooms, "boring" is the term used frequently by students to describe their typical day. Perhaps it would be wise for educators to think seriously about this and maybe even change the approach that is taken in many classes.

One approach that might leave students feeling disengaged and bored is based on the teaching philosophy that middle- and high-school classes are primarily for the acquisition of content and not necessarily for the production of knowledge. That kind of philosophy translates into a class period that is heavy on lecture, thus rendering learning a "spectator sport." Real learning, as you know, is anything but just content acquisition; learning is a constructive process that requires students to be actively engaged in what is going on. Students must become producers of their own knowledge.

Students must turn themselves into strategic thinkers, true problem solvers with the ability to apply what they learn in their classes to other settings and contexts. This will not happen if instruction mostly takes the "sit-and-git" approach. In that kind of a classroom, most likely the students will start acting out. And they will be acting out because they will be playing out their part of the ritual. Their part involves minimal involvement, minimal motivation, and minimal compliance with the rules of their classroom.

In this chapter you'll find lots of easy-to-implement strategies that will keep students active and engaged in learning. You'll also discover how you can use these strategies to differentiate instruction for many of the students you teach.

WHAT DOES THIS HAVE TO DO WITH DIFFERENTIATING INSTRUCTION ANYWAY?

Students are engaged and actively learning when students are doing. In other words, students are learning when they're the ones doing most of the work. Students need to actively solve problems, ask questions, and apply what they're learning, because when they do those things, they're making meaning and manipulating content.

Students are engaged when they are actively involved in classroom conversations and discussing information with others. They retain more when they have an opportunity to discuss information as it's presented. In other words, when students are interacting with others, their brains are more engaged.

And you can open the window even wider. When you lecture, you're addressing the auditory learners in your class. (Watch out, though. If the lecture goes on and on, even those auditory learners will begin to "fake listen" about 60 percent of the time.) When you add pictures, charts, graphs, and other similar elements to a lesson, you are appealing to the visual learners. You're also increasing retention (i.e., the length of time the average student retains the information) by as much as 38 percent for the majority of your students (Pike, 1989). When you add direct student involvement in a lesson and "hands-on" manipulation of information, you include the kinesthetic learners in your room as well. So now, instead of reaching one very narrow segment of your class, you've found a way to get everyone involved. And you're still working at the whole-group level.

WHAT'S YOUR TEACHING STYLE?

Because of the many advances in cognitive science in recent years, we now have a much better understanding of how students learn. But sometimes what we understand is one thing and what we instinctively *do* is something entirely different. (Have you ever had the experience of buying an exercise bike and setting great goals for using it because you knew it would be good for your health? And have you ever ended up using the thing as just a clothes rack? If you have, then you know exactly what I'm talking about.)

If you've been teaching for a while, you may well have been taught in traditional ways. You probably went to class, sat in a row of desks, and stared at the big person in the front of the room—the one who did almost all of the talking. Your natural tendency is to teach the way you were taught, and so you

HOLD THIS THOUGHT

I want you to remember one thing above all as you look at the strategies in this chapter: The more ways you teach, the more students you will reach!

repeat that pattern. That's natural human instinct.

Most of us also tend to teach in the way that we ourselves learn. That means that if you are a verbal/linguistic person, you may lean toward lecturing. If your strength is in computers and visuals, you may have a dynamite PowerPoint presentation that is very entertaining. But your students could still sit passively through the whole thing without talking or interacting.

If you are a very social, interpersonal kind of person, you may lean heavily on talking, organizing, and going full-steam through the material you have to get through during the term or school year. In fact, you may focus so strongly on getting through the material that you don't give enough attention to having students reflect on and process what they're learning.

The challenge in a whole-group setting of diverse learners is to avoid teaching solely in the way you were taught or the way you learn best. If you teach the way you were taught or the way you learn best, then you're unconsciously overlooking the needs of many of your students—the ones whose learning styles happen to be different from yours. Your students will be more successful if you can objectively think about your teaching style and then go beyond your own comfort zone to meet the wide range of learners in your class.

Think about it for a minute. If you took the time and energy to write down individual students' learning styles, interests, and so on, would you really be addressing the fact that your students differ? Would you be saying that you're going to do whatever it takes to engage the whole range of learners with the content you're teaching? Sure you would!

You're truly differentiating instruction in the student engagement window when you include a variety of multisensory approaches in your instruction. But you can do even better than that. As a good teacher, you know your individual students' abilities, interests, skills, and learning styles. You may not consciously think about them, and you may not have written them down, but I bet you know all of those things. The question is: what do you do with what you know?

Suppose you had a student in your class who was a strong auditory learner. Would you be willing to read (or find a volunteer to read) written work into a tape recorder or MP3

player so the student could play it back? If you felt it would truly help that student, I bet you would.

This is very different from being the "sage on the stage" and pouring your knowledge into your students. It means getting away from just covering your curriculum in the single best way you know and hoping most of the students get it.

Differentiated instruction means recognizing that learning is not a spectator sport.

IN OTHER WORDS

With all of these thoughts in mind, remember that the strategies in this chapter promote student engagement by emphasizing:

- Movement
- Interaction with others
- Interaction with the content

You cannot just pour information into the MTV-influenced, multi-media-bombarded brains of your students today. Student engagement is the only way to go!

Now, with all that as background, let's get going!

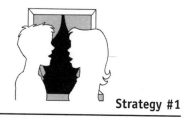

Appointment Calendar

The appointment calendar is a great way to pair off students for any activity or discussion.

STEP BY STEP

• Make one copy of the Appointment Calendar reproducible on page 102 for each student in your class.

• Give each student a copy and have him put his name on the top line.

• Have students stand up, take their appointment calendars, and find other students with whom to make appoint-

ments. Explain that each time a student makes an appointment, he should enter the appropriate name in his appointment book next to the agreed-upon time. The calendars must agree. If Ed is Matt's 9:00 AM appointment, then Matt must be Ed's 9:00 AM appointment.

• Students are responsible for keeping up with their calendars once the calendars are filled in. You might want to make a copy of each appointment calendar, though, just in case some students lose them!

Reproducible

Chapter One, Strategy #1

Appointment Calendar

NAME: Matt

Time	Name	Time	Name
8:00 a.m.	Kyle	3:30 p.m.	Michael
8:30 a.m.	Tyler	4:00 p.m.	James
9:00 a.m.	Ed	4:30 p.m.	Molly
9:30 a.m.	Jennifer	5:00 p.m.	Kate
10:00 a.m.	Sara	5:30 p.m.	Andrew
10:30 a.m.	Carter	6:00 p.m.	Jill
11:00 a.m.	Ryan	6:30 p.m.	Kim
11:30 a.m.	Cody	7:00 p.m.	Zac
12:00 noon	Amanda	7:30 p.m.	Sam
12:30 p.m.	Trevor	8:00 p.m.	Brian
1:00 p.m.	Daniel	8:30 p.m.	Jeff
1:30 p.m.	Courtney	9:00 p.m.	Ross
2:00 p.m.	Abu	9:30 p.m.	Olivia
2:30 p.m.	Whitney	10:00 p.m.	Vanessa
3:00 p.m.	Luci	10:30 p.m.	Aaron

102

Reproducible

Chapter One, Strategy #1

Appointment Calendar

NAME: Ed

Time	Name	Time	Name
8:00 a.m.	Olivia	3:30 p.m.	Abu
8:30 a.m.	Vanessa	4:00 p.m.	Whitney
9:00 a.m.	Matt	4:30 p.m.	Luci
9:30 a.m.	Aaron	5:00 p.m.	Michael
10:00 a.m.	Kyle	5:30 p.m.	James
10:30 a.m.	Tyler	6:00 p.m.	Molly
11:00 a.m.	Jennifer	6:30 p.m.	Kate
11:30 a.m.	Sara	7:00 p.m.	Andrew
12:00 noon	Carter	7:30 p.m.	Jill
12:30 p.m.	Ryan	8:00 p.m.	Kim
1:00 p.m.	Cody	8:30 p.m.	Zac
1:30 p.m.	Amanda	9:00 p.m.	Sam
2:00 p.m.	Trevor	9:30 p.m.	Brian
2:30 p.m.	Daniel	10:00 p.m.	Jeff
3:00 p.m.	Courtney	10:30 p.m.	Ross

102

• You now have a way to pair students. This comes in handy when you want students from different groups to be moving and interacting with each other. For example, in English/language arts, you might say, "Each of you please get out your appointment calendar and meet with your 2:00 PM appointment. The two of you should discuss how the novel you are currently reading depicts the era in which it was written." Or in science, you

MAKING THE CURRICULUM ACCESSIBLE

If you're going to differentiate instruction, then you must be constantly aware of the instructional needs of each student so that you can make the curriculum accessible to all students.

What do I mean by "making the curriculum accessible to all students"? Well, for a long time, we thought in terms of "modifying the curriculum." I personally like to use the phrase "making the curriculum accessible to all students." To me, that implies the intent of differentiating your instruction: to create a variety of pathways to learning, so that every student has an opportunity to be successful. The change in language reflects a new way of thinking about our students.

might say something like, "Please meet with your 4:00 PM appointment and discuss how humans cause chemical and physical weathering."

• When you look at the reproducible for the appointment book, you'll notice that times are listed all the way up to 10:30 at night. Don't worry. It's not that differentiating means you'll have to extend the school day until 10:30 PM. The times in the appointment books are just a way of identifying who's paired with whom for a particular activity. It may be 10:00 in the morning when you ask students to meet with their 9:00 PM appointments.

• Want to build on this strategy? If you ask each student to walk at least seven steps to find a partner, that extra bit of exercise will get more oxygen to that student's brain. And that can help get rid of those mental cobwebs.

• To make the curriculum even more accessible in this case, you may want to strategically select a few of the partners yourself. For example, you might be the one who identifies the 1:30 PM partners in the room. You might arrange for stronger students to be paired with weaker ones, so that later you can ask students to meet with their 1:30 PM partners and have them read dialog from a play to each other. The stronger student would go first to provide modeling and support; then the weaker student would take his turn.

VARIATION

Instead of pairing weaker and stronger students, you can arrange, say, the 9:00 AM appointments to pair off students who are at the same level of understanding. Only you will know how you strategically selected the pairings. You can then make sure each pair is reading materials at the appropriate level of difficulty.

NOW LOOK WHAT YOU'VE DONE!

You've differentiated for a specific learning modality. This strategy is great for those bodily/kinesthetic learners, and that's a help for them *and* you. If you don't give those kids legitimate ways to move, they'll find their own ways—and you may not be so happy with the times they pick! This approach gives them a purpose for moving around.

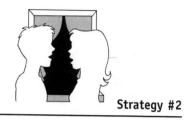

Timed-Pair Paraphrase

Instead of just asking students to think about a topic and share their thoughts, go one step further and time each student's sharing. This approach, which encourages participation by *all* students, is adapted from a couple of cooperative learning structures (Kagan, 1994, 1998). It's a simple strategy that can make a big difference.

STEP BY STEP

- Ask each student to refer to his appointment calendar (see page 17) and meet with a specific appointment partner. (Tell students to meet with their 1:00 PM appointment partners, for example.)

- When students have found their partners, say, "Decide which of you is A and which of you is B. I want A to share with B ways in which a character from the novel you're reading is similar to and different from someone he knows. You have two minutes. B, if your partner quits sharing, ask questions."

- Set a timer. After two (or any number) of minutes, ask B to paraphrase what he heard A share. The paraphrase might start, "I heard you say . . ." (This will improve those listening skills!)

- Ask several Bs to share with the class what their partners said.

- Reverse the process so that each A can share with each B. Then ask several As to share with the rest of the class.

NOW LOOK WHAT YOU'VE DONE!

There's a specific reason you are structuring the sharing by timing each student. You know you have those "hogs" and "logs" in your classroom. If you just ask the students to engage in a discussion, the hog will talk the entire time and the log will check out and think about what's for lunch. A Timed-Pair Paraphrase lets you control that.

By using this strategy, you're helping the log to be successful because you're inviting her into the discussion. You're also differentiating, because part of differentiating is knowing each student and then opening a pathway to success for that student.

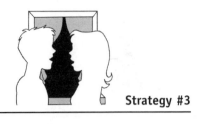

Carousel Your Way Through a K–W–L

What do you do when you try to use a K–W–L (What I Know, What I Want to Know, What I Learned) strategy with your class and it just flops? Maybe you ask your students, "What do you know about the Gettysburg Address?" and they say, "Nothing." You say, "What would you like to know?" and they say, "Nothing." You think, "This is the most unmotivated group I've ever had!"

Maybe there's a solution. Part of making a commitment to differentiating instruction is making a commitment to being a responsive teacher. Instead of blaming the students, ask yourself what you could do to make the K–W–L strategy a little more interactive.

One way is to turn it into a carousel.

STEP BY STEP

- Decide on the major topics students will cover during a particular unit and write each one of those topics on a separate sheet of chart paper; then post each sheet of chart paper in a different area of the classroom. If students are studying Expansionism, you might post three charts: one headed "Louisiana Purchase," one headed "Lewis & Clark Expedition," and one headed "Manifest Destiny."

- Divide students into the same number of groups as there are charts hanging in the room (in this example, three).

- Give each group a marker in a different color, and ask those students to go to one of the charts.

- Ask each group to appoint a recorder. The recorder's job is to list on the chart the things the members of the group think they know about the topic.

- After a few minutes, have each group rotate to another chart. Ask the group to review what the other students already wrote on that chart, put a checkmark (with their colored marker) beside those things they also knew about the topic, and then make their own additions to the list.

- Tell the students that, at this point, they should just ignore anything they think is wrong. Reassure them that as they read and study the material, it will become clearer whether anything needs to be changed.

- Keep this up until all students are back at the charts where they started. Now ask each group to select a reporter.

- Give each group a few minutes to look over all the information now on their chart. Then ask each reporter to give the class a brief verbal summary of the information on the chart her group started.

- After each group reports, ask the class to think of some questions they have about each of the topics. List these in writing on additional sheets of chart paper so that all the students can see and refer to them during their study.

* After they complete the unit of study, have students return to the charts and discuss—both within their original groups and with the entire class—what they've learned.

NOW LOOK WHAT YOU'VE DONE!

You've gotten students up and moving around, which helps the kinesthetic learners. You've got them talking and listening, which helps the auditory learners. And you've got them making lists, which helps the visual learners. Hey, you're differentiating!

FOR STUDENTS WHO ALREADY KNOW THE TOPIC

What if, during the carousel recording of "What We Know About the Topic," you observe several students who already seem to know even more than you do? You know the students I'm talking about—the ones who could easily sub for you when you're absent—and do a good job!

Try having those students opt out of some of the other activities associated with this unit and work on independent projects related to the unit of study. For example, ask each of those students to select a specific in-depth question the class has come up with, research that question, and then make a presentation to the class.

Show—Don't Tell

One of the best ways for students to learn vocabulary is to associate each new word with a visual or with movement. All of your students will get into this student-centered vocabulary strategy, but it's especially good for those visual/spatial learners and bodily/kinesthetic learners. This strategy works very well for learning content-specific terms, too. Use it to reinforce chemical symbols in chemistry classes or geologic ages in earth science. It's also a good strategy for teaching parts of speech in English or vocabulary in a foreign-language class.

STEP BY STEP

• Give each student a list that shows the vocabulary words the class is studying and the definitions of those words.

• Give each student an index card with one of the words on it, plus a large piece of paper and a bunch of markers in assorted colors.

• Tell the class that each student should draw a picture of her word and then figure out a way to act out that word. (Drawing the words forces students to *think* about meanings, not just memorize them.) Explain that each student needs to do this without showing other students the word on her card.

• Have each student (or several selected students) come to the front of the room,

show the class his picture, and act out his word. For example, let's say you give a student a card with the word "meticulous," and the list of definitions says that "meticulous" means "exacting, precise." A student might draw a messy room with a slash through it to show an antonymic meaning, and his action might be to organize several items on a desk very carefully.

• Ask the other students to guess the word. Once they've figured it out, have all the students repeat the action.

• Each time a student comes to the front and acts out a word, follow up by leading the class in a review of all the words presented so far. To do this, have the class say each word and act out the motion.

• At the end of the session, collect all the pictures.

• The next day, for a quick review, show each picture and have students act out the word associated with that picture.

NOW LOOK WHAT YOU'VE DONE!

By offering your students multiple pathways to success, you've opened up the learning process to a much wider range of learners. And that means you've given students a much greater chance of working those vocabulary words into long-term memory.

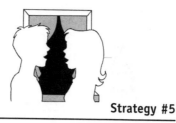

That's Me!

This strategy offers a great way to build community in your classroom and to get students acquainted with each other at the beginning of the school year. It also gets students moving, because you're asking them to do more than just raise their hands.

STEP BY STEP

- Explain to your students that you're going to make a statement such as any of the following:

  ✓ "I love _____ [name a popular musical group]."

  ✓ "My favorite television show is _____."

  ✓ "I play _____ [name a sport]."

  ✓ "My birthday is in January."

  ✓ "I hate homework."

- Tell students that when you make a statement, anyone for whom that statement is true should stand and say, "That's me!"

NOW LOOK WHAT YOU'VE DONE!

An important part of working together in a differentiated classroom is building a community of learners. When you structure activities that give students a chance to get to know one another, they get some insight into other students with whom they have things in common.

FOR LATER IN THE YEAR

Come back to this activity later in the year and give it a slight twist. This time, tell students that you'll be making statements related to topics they've been studying. Statements might be something like these:

"I know two possible explanations for _____."

"I know how _____ is related to _____."

"I know how _____ [book title] explores the theme _____."

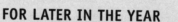

"I can summarize _____."

This time, those students who know the answer should stand and say, "That's me!" Then you can call on one or two students to give the answers.

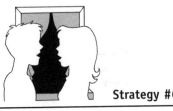

Snowball Fight

This activity involves movement and engages students. It can be used for reviewing, predicting, summarizing learning, and more. And if you live in the South, like me, this may be the closest you and some of your students ever get to seeing snow!

STEP BY STEP

- Let's say you'd like students to reflect on the day's course content. Ask each student to put his name on a piece of paper and then to write on that paper something learned in class that day. Encourage students to write clearly so that someone else can read what they've written.

THE BUTTON PUSHER

What do you do about the student who writes, "I learned nothing"? That student is probably trying to "push your buttons," so you might just say, "Well, I bet tomorrow you'll learn something." Later you might reconnect with that student to discuss what the problem is.

Other times maybe you'd rather address the issue of kids thinking they aren't learning anything when they really are. It can make for a great discussion to have the whole class talk about what they've learned.

- Have students bring their papers and form a large circle.

- Tell students that each of them should wad her paper up into a ball. On your signal, they should all throw their papers into the center of the circle. Then each student should grab somebody else's "snowball" from the pile and throw it into the center of the circle.

- Continue this "snowball fight" for as long as you can stand it (like about one minute), and then signal for the students to stop.

- Have each student pick up any "snowball" that has landed close by.

- Call on a few students to read to the rest of the class the contents of the "snowballs" they've found. Be sure to comment on the lessons/facts written on the papers. For correct information you might say something like, "I can tell you were really listening today." For incorrect information, you might say something like, "Interesting thought. Let's discuss it a minute."

- Collect all "snowballs" for assessment purposes.

VARIATIONS

Variation 1: For a daily review, choose three to five topics from things the class is studying. These could be radioactive elements, Impressionist painters, Constitutional Amendments, or whatever. Write one of these topics at the top of each of several pieces of paper, then do the same with each of the other topics you've chosen. Wad up the pieces of paper and toss them on the floor. Have each student grab a snowball and open it up, then write on the paper his name and something he learned about that topic. Toss the snowballs again and then repeat the process as above.

Variation 2: If you're reluctant to encourage your students to throw anything, try this alternative. Give the first student in each row a piece of paper with a topic written on it. Each person in the row must write her name and something she learned about that topic, fold the paper like a fan so the next person can't see what was written, and then pass the folded paper on to her neighbor. Repeat until the papers get to the ends of the rows, where you collect them. This can give you a strong basis for a classroom discussion.

NOW LOOK WHAT YOU'VE DONE!

In addition to student engagement, this also incorporates another aspect of differentiating: using ongoing assessment to drive your instruction. If a student gives an incorrect response—or no response at all—on the paper, that tells you this student needs some extra instruction. If he writes "Beats me!" that's a pretty good clue, too!

TIPS FOR GIVING DIRECTIONS

You give your students directions every day. But do they often look at you like you're an alien? Try these quick tips for making sure they're understanding what it is you're asking them to do.

- Never assume that your students know what to do just because you've given them directions. Always check for their understanding. One way to do this is to ask them to turn to a neighbor and give the directions in their own words.

- Phrase questions about directions or procedures in ways that elicit specific student responses. Instead of saying, "Does everyone have a book?" say, "Raise your hand if you need a book."

- Talk directly to those students who are being asked to do something: "Those in group 1, go to the front of the room."

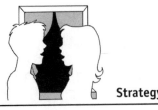

Vote with Your Feet & Not Your Hands

The title of this strategy does not mean that your students stand on their hands to vote. Rather, they're going to move to one side of the classroom or another to agree or disagree with a statement. This strategy—useful for clarifying values and stimulating thinking—works for defining views on everything from evolution to pollution issues to capital punishment. It's guaranteed to energize and engage your students.

STEP BY STEP

- Make a statement such as, "Students should be required to wear uniforms to school."

- Tell students that they should move to one side of the room if they agree with the statement and to the opposite side if they disagree.

- Ask individual students to explain and elaborate on their viewpoints. Be sure to accept all answers and encourage a discussion. You might want to time the discussion.

VARIATION

After completing this activity, keep "Agree" and "Disagree" signs posted at opposite ends of the room all year long. This can help to facilitate further discussions as you continue to move through the curriculum.

NOW LOOK WHAT YOU'VE DONE!

In a differentiated classroom, you want students to be thinking and doing. When you ask them a question that has no single correct answer, the question becomes an invitation to think. You've engaged students' minds. If you ask them to get up out of their seats and stand on one side of the room to vote, you've got their bodies engaged as well. And the struggling learners in your class may get an added benefit: hearing the thinking of others sometimes can help struggling learners to develop their own thought processes.

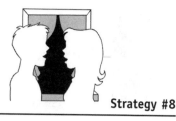

What's My Name?

Here's a fun, active way to do a quick review, get students up and moving, and reinforce learning.

STEP BY STEP

- Give each student a stick-on name tag, but don't write the student's name on it. Instead, use content from a unit of study. For example, give each student a name tag with a chemical symbol written on it.

- Have students walk around the room learning the new "names" of their classmates. If Aaron's name tag is the one that says, "Fe," then Aaron's new name is "Iron." Have students call one another by their new names for as long as you think it's appropriate.

- This can also give you an opportunity to do some one-on-one teaching while everyone else is engaged in the activity. Let's say you know that Tim really doesn't know the chemical symbols. You get in the game by wearing several name tags with those symbols that Tim doesn't know. You make sure that Tim has to call you by all your names. You also prompt him as necessary.

VARIATIONS

Variation 1: This works for other areas of the curriculum, too. In math, name tags could include dodecahedrons, trapezoids, cones, and other geometric shapes. Or how about using food names when teaching a foreign language? Can't you just see somebody whose name is "churrasco" or "pescado" for the day?

Variation 2: Divide the class in half. Give each student in one group an index card on which you've written a chemical symbol. Each student in the other group gets a card with the name of a corresponding element. Have students circulate around the room, matching names and symbols.

NOW LOOK WHAT YOU'VE DONE!

You've engaged all your students and given them a chance to review content in a physically active way. At the same time, you've been able to give a little extra coaching to a student who needs it.

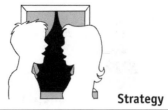

Circle the Category

Used either before or after reading, this strategy helps students to develop vocabulary and to organize and categorize information. It has another use, too. If your students find that creating the outline is the hardest part of writing a research paper, try this approach to give them some practice in organizing information.

STEP BY STEP

- Give each student an index card.

- Ask each student to write on the card one word pertaining to a topic the class has studied or is about to study. If the class has been learning about types of government, a student might write "oligarchy" on the index card.

- Have students get up and move about the room comparing index cards. Then ask them to cluster into groups according to how they think words might go together. For example, students with "oligarchy," "dictatorship," and "monar-

Governments That Are Not Elected

A MANAGEMENT TIP

Be very specific about when movement in the room is acceptable and expect students to move quickly into various groups. You might set an overhead TeachTimer and require students to be in groups by the time the timer goes off, or when music stops, or when you give a set signal. TeachTimers are available from Crystal Springs Books (www.crystalsprings.com).

ocracies

NOW LOOK WHAT YOU'VE DONE!

You've taught categorization, you've fostered higher-level thinking, and—if you asked students to use this strategy before they read the material—you've gained an opportunity to find out what they knew or didn't know about the topic you were about to study.

HERE'S YOUR PRE-ASSESSMENT

In some cases you might find that, before they study a particular topic, some of the students are unable to generate any words relating to that topic. In that case, you can generate some appropriate words and write them on the index cards yourself. On the other hand, some students may ask for more index cards. (If they ask for more cards, give 'em more cards!)

chy" on their index cards might decide to stand together.

- Once students have grouped themselves, give each group a large sheet of paper and a marker and ask them to write a label for their cluster of words. The oligarchy-dictatorship-monarchy group might decide the label for their cluster is "Governments That Are Not Elected."

- Have one student hold the paper while the rest of the group makes a circle around him. Then ask each group to choose one member to explain to the rest of the class why the group clustered together and why they chose their particular label.

VARIATION

After the class reads a novel, write the characters' names on the index cards and have the students group them by character traits.

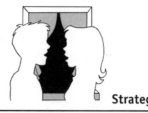

Milling to Music

This is a quick and very flexible way to incorporate movement and student engagement in any lesson.

STEP BY STEP

Tell students you're going to play some music (upbeat music works best) and that when the music starts, you want them to get up and mill about the classroom.

- Explain that when you stop the music, students are to freeze.

- When the music stops and the students freeze, ask them a question that requires a number as an answer. For example, you might say, "What is the square root of sixteen?"

- Have students quickly get into groups. Since the answer in this case was four, they'd get into groups of four. If some students are left over, tell them they are in the "lost and found" and ask them to join any group. On the next round, ask students to make sure those students are included in a group first.

- Now give students any content to discuss. They could talk about methods for solving quadratic equations. They could discuss the causes of World War I. They could examine why astronomers redefined Pluto's status in our solar system.

- Put yourself in the mixing and milling as well. Position yourself so that when you ask the question, you're in close proximity to a student or students who are either struggling with content or ready for a higher-level discussion. If you make sure you get to talk with that student or students, you'll have a perfect opportunity for some small-group reteaching or, perhaps, a more in-depth discussion of content.

- After a few minutes, start the music again. Once again have students mill about the room and then freeze when you stop the music. Repeat the rest of the process, having the students form different-sized groups by varying the questions you ask. If you ask, "What is 45 divided by 15?" then students would form groups of three.

NOW LOOK WHAT YOU'VE DONE!

Just having students move to music is not differentiation. It might be novel or a break in the routine for the class period, but it's not differentiation. If you're listening to what students are sharing and if you're gathering information to make instructional decisions based on student responses, however, then you are differentiating.

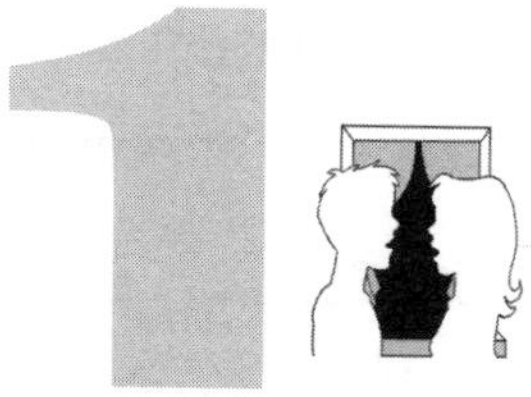

Now It's Your Turn to Reflect on This Chapter

Are you encouraged that you can begin your journey into differentiating in a whole-group setting with some of these strategies? Keep in mind the fact that in a whole-group setting, we need to do more than just talk to students if we want them to attain personal mastery of concepts, gain real understanding, and develop skills. As you begin to differentiate instruction in your whole-group setting, a good first step is to think about how you can engage all of your students while also creating different pathways for those who need that additional support.

I'd like to suggest you stop now and take the time for some reflection and action planning. Why am I asking you to make some specific plans? Well, if you don't spend a few minutes in reflection and action planning, chances are you'll put this book down and go to your other life (pick up a child, cook dinner, go to a meeting, etc.) or you'll start doing schoolwork (grading papers, making lesson plans, etc). Then when you decide to pick up this book again, you will have forgotten what you read.

On the other hand, if you spend a few minutes reflecting and planning after you read each chapter, then you can quickly look and see what had the most impact on you as you read. You're creating your plan. (I'm differentiating a little for you and your needs now!) So, pick up a pen or pencil and fill in the blanks.

What is your "aha!" or insight or thinking after reading this chapter?

_____

_____

_____

_____

What strategy will you try first? How will you use it in your classroom?

_____

_____

_____

_____

_____

_____

How and why might you tailor one of the strategies in this chapter to meet the needs of a specific student or students?

_____

_____

_____

_____

_____

_____

_____

_____

2

Questioning Window

You may be wondering why in the world this book would include a chapter on questioning. It's not news that questioning is an important part of teaching. But think about this a minute. In your classroom, you're at the mercy of a bell that rings every 45, 55, 75, or 90 minutes. As soon as the bell rings, that class leaves and another one appears. You want to do a good job, and you want all of your students to be successful, but you have to manage that in those 45-, 55-, 75-, or 90-minute blocks.

So you fall into the habit of viewing yourself as the one who must move the instruction forward. If a student asks a question, that's an interruption; there just isn't enough time in a class period for a lot of questions. As a result, you become the main question asker.

Then you begin to think that the main goal of asking questions at all is to assess the performance of the students. If that's the case, you decide (consciously or not) that maybe questions are best left to a quiz at the end of a unit or the end of a class period. You go on to assume that during class, there is time only to ask students if everyone understands or if anybody has any questions. Heaven forbid that somebody *does* have a question—that would surely interrupt the learning process!

But what if that *is* the learning process?

Have you ever asked your class, "Are there any questions?" and had students just sit there and stare at you in total silence? Have you ever asked, "Does everyone understand?" and had students bob their heads up and down? You probably think everything about your instruction is very clear to your students. But do you know what the head bobbing really means?

It means their neck muscles are moving.

That's all it means. What those students are really thinking, if they are engaged at all, is that if you continue teaching, then they will begin to understand at some point.

In a setting like this, students become reluctant to interrupt you and ask questions. In a whole-group setting, it's easy to de-emphasize questioning and to let it become a secondary vehicle of your instruction. The primary vehicle is you, the "sage on the stage,"

constantly reconstructing a text or problem for your students. You, not the students, are creating an understanding of the content that goes beyond just the surface.

STUDENT-CENTERED INSTRUCTION

But remember: differentiation is student centered and not teacher centered. Exactly what does "student centered" mean? It means the focus is off you and on your students. It means students are doing something, as opposed to just sitting and listening.

Please don't misunderstand me. I'm not suggesting you're doing things wrong. But I *am* suggesting that instruction in your whole-group setting will be even more effective if you give more thought to the questioning that takes place—both the questions you ask and the questions the students generate.

Good questioning engages students, helps them construct meaning, and develops higher-level thinking skills. How can your students remember and use what they're learn-

ing if the only time they open their mouths is to yawn? (Of course, yawning is exactly what you'll get if your primary vehicle for instruction is teacher talk!)

That brings me to another consideration: which do you think is more important in your classroom, the question or the answer?

You might say, "Well, I present the curriculum to the whole class in the best way I know how, and the majority of them can answer the questions I ask. I've taught it, and I assume that if they answer my questions, they've learned it. So the answer is more important."

But what if I said to you that there is more thinking and learning going on when students are asking questions?

Consider entrepreneur and inventor George Ballas of Houston, Texas. For years, Mr. Ballas was frustrated because he couldn't get rid of the weeds that grew around the trunks of the trees in his yard. He had gone through school and played the question-and-answer game, just as I did and just as you probably did. He learned how to give the answers the teacher wanted. However, Mr. Ballas was a little different from the rest of us.

He also asked the question.

When he was having his car washed one day, Mr. Ballas noticed how the car-wash brushes washed all around the outside of his car, managing to clean the car without damaging it. So he asked himself, "Is there something I could make that would operate on this same concept—something that would help me get rid of the weeds around the trunks of my trees without damaging the trees?"

George Ballas is the inventor of the Weedeater string trimmer. Millions of Americans have Weedeater trimmers to help keep their yards looking nice—and Mr. Ballas has millions of dollars in the bank! Before I purchased a Weedeater, I was frustrated with the weeds in my yard just as Mr. Ballas had been. But I didn't ask the question.

Think about it. Any innovator—in education, the arts, architecture, science, engineering, business, or weed trimming—has to ask questions, to seek in order to drive discovery. Too many of our students have become information oriented rather than thinking oriented. We need to teach them to ask the question.

THE QUESTION IS MORE IMPORTANT THAN THE ANSWER

But you know what research has shown? On average, teachers ask 80 questions each hour. Can you guess how many questions students ask in that same time period?

Two.

Yep, two (Kagan, 1999). And that's two questions for the entire class, so that means most kids aren't asking *any* questions. There are reasons why that happens, and we've talked about them already. So my point is this: Think about what an opportunity you have as a teacher! If you can force yourself to ask for *questions* from your students instead of always calling for answers, think how much more they could learn!

By the way, have you noticed that when the students are the ones coming up with the questions, they're automatically differentiating themselves? For example, when studying capital punishment, a struggling student might ask, "What is capital punishment?" and a more advanced student might ask, "Could we talk about whether capital punishment is right? Here's what I think and I can support my view."

Of course there still will be times when you do need to be the one asking the questions. Those are the times when you need to think about something else: the kinds of questions you're asking. Remember when you were in school and you learned about Bloom's Taxonomy? You probably studied the different levels of thinking, and somebody probably

drummed it into your head that you need to emphasize the questions from the higher end of the scale.

You remember those higher-level questions, right? The synthesis and evaluation questions that require students to understand and apply information? As opposed to the knowledge and comprehension questions that call for memorized answers?

Those higher-level thinking skills are more important today than ever, for a reason Benjamin Bloom would never have thought of: more and more of them are showing up on accountability assessments. Knowing that, can you guess what kinds of questions teachers are asking their students?

Research has shown that, in classrooms all across America, 80 percent of the questions teachers ask are still at the knowledge and comprehension level (Johnson, 1996).

So here's another opportunity. If you can get yourself to ask higher-level questions, and

if you can get your students to ask and answer questions at a higher level, think about how much more learning you'll be able to get out of your class time.

WHAT DOES THIS HAVE TO DO WITH DIFFERENTIATING INSTRUCTION ANYWAY?

There's a story that a teacher once asked a student to summarize the life of Socrates in four sentences. The student replied: "Socrates lived a long time ago. He was very intelligent. Socrates gave long speeches. His listeners poisoned him."

Maybe there's a lesson here. Often teachers tend to "talk at" students because that approach is easier and seems more efficient. It's the way many of us were taught, and it's more organized. However, if more learning occurs when more questioning occurs, and if all of your students need to be pushed to think and process at higher levels, maybe there's a better alternative.

As you consider the wide range of learners in your classroom, sometimes it's appropriate to ask the struggling students questions that simplify the content and to ask the more able students those higher-level questions. For example, you might ask one student to list the key elements of the U.S. Civil Rights movement and another student to compare and contrast that movement with the struggle to end Apartheid in South Africa.

Let's take it another step. If the question is more important than the answer, then students need to learn to generate questions. Good readers are always asking questions while reading. They're engaged and active while reading, not passively waiting for the teacher to ask the questions at the end. The ability to generate questions is the key to higher levels of learning.

Students can pose questions that come from their interests in content, and you can use those questions to help the students set goals for learning. For example, a student might want to know why certain antibiotics are used to treat certain diseases, why some antibiotics are called "broad spectrum," and how common it is for some antibiotics to cause allergic reactions.

This chapter will give you some easy-to-implement strategies for both the questions you ask and the ones the students generate. But before you continue, I have one other suggestion for you. Try asking a colleague to videotape one of your lessons so you can see how effective your questioning is now. Once you've established that baseline, open this window by turning the page and considering the strategies that follow.

The Parking Lot & Geometric Questions

Thinking takes time. In the next strategy, we'll look at the wait time you give your students after you ask a question. The Parking Lot and Geometric Questions give your students wait time for *coming up with* questions and more wait time before you respond. This can particularly benefit certain students from poverty, some English language learners, some boys, and some students with identified learning disabilities.

STEP BY STEP

- Make copies of one or both of the Parking Lot and Geometric Questions reproducibles on pages 103–104.

- Give those copies to your students to keep in their notebooks. If you're using the Parking Lot reproducible, note that some students drive to school and park their cars there. Explain that now you're giving them an opportunity to park their questions.

- During a unit of study, have students write on those copies any questions or observations they have about the topic.

- Reserve the last part of your class time to respond to all unresolved questions.

VARIATION

Instead of making copies for students to keep, enlarge the reproducibles on a copier, laminate them, and use them as classroom posters. Then have students write their questions on sticky notes and stick them on the posters. You can even have them use different colors of notes for different categories: when reading novels, for example, maybe have them use pink for questions about characterization, yellow for symbolism, and so on.

NOW LOOK WHAT YOU'VE DONE!

When you allow students to have wait time, you're modeling for them that thinking is valued in the classroom.

Differentiated Wait Time

You had the class in your teacher preparation that told you it was important to give students "wait time" after asking a question. Why is that important? Thinking takes time. That doesn't fit well with the pressure you feel today to get in so much instruction in a limited time. The pressure leads to a hurried pace of instruction, and that, in turn, leads to a harried environment. Before you realize it, you're firing questions at your students one right after the other.

I know that in my classroom, because I like to keep things moving, I probably gave my students only a couple of seconds of wait time. What's worse is that I probably answered most of the questions I asked my students.

I'll just blame it on my husband. Sometimes when he's slow to answer, I'll answer for him. That behavior became a habit that carried over to the students. Does this sound familiar to you—in your home *or* your classroom? Husbands are probably glad they don't have to respond, but our students are different. Although they might be glad they don't *have* to respond, many students are *unable* to respond if they don't have sufficient wait time. As soon as somebody answers the question, everybody else stops thinking.

Finding creative ways to add some wait time to your questioning can make a big difference. That's where this strategy comes in.

TAKE YOUR CHOICE

- **Time to think:** Give students 5 to 10 seconds to respond to a question. Make sure they know that they're expected to use that time to think about their answers.

- **Random selection:** Follow an unpredictable approach to calling on students. For example, put each student's name on an index card. Call on students at random, pulling a card from the deck and replacing it somewhere in the deck after the student has responded. That means some students might be called on more than once. It also means students learn they're all responsible for every question.

- **Hands up:** Tell students you're not going to call on anyone until more than half of them have raised their hands. This steers the class away from the situation in which a handful of dominant (and sometimes domineering) students always chime in.

- **Hands down:** Occasionally call on students who don't have their hands raised.

- **Explanation please:** Ask students to explain how they arrived at their responses, whether or not the responses are correct. It's the thinking you're after.

VARIATIONS

Variation 1: You can use the index-card approach as an assessment tool, too. When you call on a student, put a check plus (correct), a check (attempt), or a check minus (refused) on the back of the card, depending on the response of the student. After about two or three days, turn the cards over and call on students based on the checks. Again, all students participate.

Variation 2: Set up three unmarked cans for the index cards. Place all the cards in one can initially, and then move them to the other two cans based on students' responses. For example: suppose you draw Bob's card. If he answers the question correctly, you place his card in what you know is the "mastery can." If he answers incorrectly or not at all, his card goes in the "reteach can," indicating that he needs additional review with the teacher or a peer helper.

NOW LOOK WHAT YOU'VE DONE!

When you begin to increase wait time in your whole-group setting, you'll notice that the length of student responses increases and failure to respond decreases. When you become less and less the sage on the stage, students ask more questions and begin to interact with one another. You'll find yourself asking questions at a higher level, especially of those students who can handle that. Also, you'll find that your students make more inferences, and they start giving more speculative responses. Speculative responses boost creative thinking.

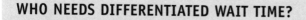

WHO NEEDS DIFFERENTIATED WAIT TIME?

While additional wait time will increase the quality and depth of the answers in general, some wait time may need to be differentiated. Often boys need more wait time than girls. Some students from poverty need more wait time because they have less background knowledge and more limited vocabulary. Often English-language learners need additional time to process thoughts in their first language and then to translate into English. Many students with identified learning disabilities need additional time to process and reflect before giving a response.

But what about those students at the other end of the spectrum—the ones you perceive to be highly able? It may surprise you to know that retrieval rates and intelligence are not linked. Sometimes those highly able students in your room have neural networks that are much denser, and their thoughts and responses are more complex (Kingore, 2004). If you call only on the students whose hands are up in the air first, you and your class will miss the deeper thoughts of some of these students.

I Do Have a Question

Here's a strategy that encourages students to ask questions during a class discussion. It also gives you a good way to make sure you're asking questions that go beyond just the knowledge and comprehension levels of questioning.

STEP BY STEP

- Use the Key Words & Sample Questions from Bloom's Taxonomy reproducible on pages 105–106 to create questions for a unit of study.

- Write a different question on each of several index cards, making sure to include questions from the higher levels.

- Select several students at random and give each of them one of the cards. (You don't have to be secretive about this. The other students are sure to figure out what you're doing anyway!)

- Tell each of those students that when he hears you say, "Does anyone have a question?" that's his cue to raise his hand.

- Be sure to include those "plants" as you call on students to ask the questions.

NOW LOOK WHAT YOU'VE DONE!

Shouldn't one of our long-term goals for students be for them to learn how to ask questions and continue developing new ways of thinking? By "planting" questions that invite higher-level thinking, you engage more students because they're manipulating and relating to the content rather than just repeating the content by rote. These kinds of whole-class discussions also serve as models so that students who aren't yet ready to answer at a higher level can benefit from the discussion.

Question Stems & Cubing

We know that different students have different learning preferences. The way you structure questions can instantly exclude some of your students, or it can invite all of them into the process. To be sure you're including everyone, try beginning your questions with a variety of question stems and using a strategy known as cubing.

Cubing uses a simple visual of an easily constructed cube to approach a topic from multiple directions. You can use cubes in different colors to differentiate according to learning modalities.

STEP BY STEP

• First you need to know how many of each kind of cube you're going to make for your class. To figure that out, think about how you'd group your students according to learning modalities. Working from the premise that each group will have no more than four students, you need to know how many groups of visual learners you have, how many groups of auditory learners, and how many groups of kinesthetic learners.

• Turn to the reproducibles on pages 107–109. Each section of each of these cube patterns

has a command. You'll need to add specific instructions to the commands to create appropriate tasks for each group. But don't do that yet.

• Since you may want to come back and re-use the cube patterns later, I'd suggest that your next step should be to make one copy of each of the three learning-styles cube patterns on plain white paper. You might want to enlarge these on the copier in order to have more room to write.

FOR EXAMPLE

If the class is studying genetics, then you might create a cube for visual learners on which the sides read something like this:

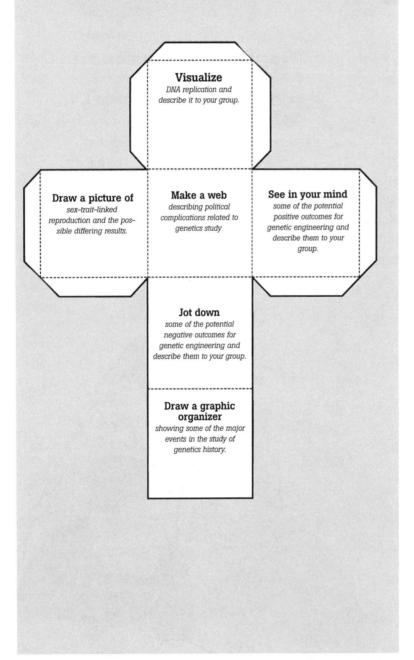

Visualize
DNA replication and describe it to your group.

Draw a picture of
sex-trait-linked reproduction and the possible differing results.

Make a web
describing political complications related to genetics study.

See in your mind
some of the potential positive outcomes for genetic engineering and describe them to your group.

Jot down
some of the potential negative outcomes for genetic engineering and describe them to your group.

Draw a graphic organizer
showing some of the major events in the study of genetics history.

• Next, on your copies, add specific task instructions to each section of each cube.

• Go back to the copier with the filled-in cube patterns. Make the appropriate number of cube patterns for each learning modality, using a different color of card stock for each type of cube. Let's say you copy the cube for visual learners onto green card stock, the one for auditory learners onto blue stock, and the one for kinesthetic learners onto yellow stock.

• In class, divide the students into the groups you've decided on. Give each group a cube in the appropriate color. Make sure the students understand what each command means.

• Have the students in each group take turns throwing the cube and noting the instructions listed on the part of the cube that lands face up. Explain that if the student doesn't want to perform that task, he can roll the cube a second time.

• Explain that once each student knows what his task is, he should work on that assignment on his own. However, students can also help each other.

• Finally, ask students to share with one another how they completed their tasks.

VARIATIONS

Variation 1: Start with the blank Cube Pattern reproducible on page 110 and create new cubes that differentiate according to student interests.

Variation 2: Give unassembled cubes to individual students, asking each student to respond to all six commands and assemble the cube.

Variation 3: On each cube, include commands that will appeal to different modalities. Create heterogeneous groups of students.

Allow the students to work together to discuss, delegate, make decisions, and complete the work. When students who have strengths in different modalities work together, they learn to stretch themselves in new ways.

NOW LOOK WHAT YOU'VE DONE!

You've used the same strategy for the whole group, but you've varied the details to honor each modality preference. As a result, you've dramatically increased each student's chance to become engaged in learning—and that means you've also increased his chances of succeeding.

AN INTERNET CONNECTION

One way to find out more about how your students learn best is to have them take a learning styles test on the Internet, such as the one at www.ldpride.net. You might give extra credit to each student who takes the test and turns it in with a written paragraph explaining what she thinks of the test and giving her analysis of whether she thinks it's accurate or not. This then gives you the information you need to differentiate by learning style.

Cubing & Bloom's

The previous strategy addressed ways to reach different learning modalities through the cubing strategy. You can also create cubes in which the instructions on each side of the cube correspond to one level of Bloom's Taxonomy. This is a great way to build higher-level thinking skills.

STEP BY STEP

- For a cube pattern, turn to the Bloom's Cube reproducible on page 111.

- Since you may want to come back and re-use the cube pattern later with other content, make one copy of the pattern on plain white paper. (You might want to use the enlarging feature on the copier in order to give yourself more room to write.)

- See how there are six sides to the pattern, and how each side of the cube pattern has a command? And you know how Bloom's Taxonomy deals with six levels of thinking? I'm so glad Ben made this easy for us! What you're going to do is add specific instructions to each basic command so that you create an appropriate task for each level of thinking.

- To help students understand the process, try modeling this strategy first with a non-academic topic. For example, make a cube using the commands in the box on this page and based on the subject of the class you're teaching (e.g., "Describe what

THE BLOOM'S CUBE

You can make a cube to encourage higher-level thinking by starting with these commands on the six sides of the cube:

Describe . . . (knowledge level)

Explain . . . (comprehension level)

Develop . . . (application level)

Classify . . . (analysis level)

Create a new . . . (synthesis level)

In your opinion . . . (evaluation level)

For example, suppose a class is studying the impact of the Internet on the democratization of access to information. The sides of the cube might read:

- Describe the different ways the Internet has changed how information is obtained and propagated.

- Explain how you surveyed other students, teachers, the administration, and community members about their use of MySpace, Wikipedia, blogs, etc.

- Develop a graph showing the effects of our shift into the Information Age.

- Classify the problems we face in terms of the way we use information, check its reliability, and provide access to its creation and communication.

- Create solutions to some of the problems we face with information overload and management.

- In your opinion, has the Internet created more space for democracy and the sharing of ideas and information?

this class is about," "In your opinion, how important is the subject of this class?" etc.). Have students take turns rolling the cube and giving responses, or write the six commands on the board and work with them from there. You might get some interesting results!

- Once you're sure students understand the process, you can apply the same principle to the content your class is studying. Go back to the copier with the same or another filled-in cube pattern and make enough copies so that you can give one to each student in the class.

- Hand out the copies to students and explain that each student is to respond to each of the six prompts independently (on the cube itself, if she has enough room there, or on a separate sheet of paper if she needs more space). However, anyone can also ask for help from other students or from you if he needs it.

- Ask students to share with one another how they completed their responses.

- Now try out this strategy for yourself! Using the command prompts from the box on page 44, think about your responses to each of the six commands. Your topic is differentiating instruction in a whole-group setting.

VARIATION

Try color coding the Bloom's cubes. Start with the same reproducible, but make extra copies. Fill in the sides of each color-coded copy with commands that are appropriate for the various readiness levels, interests, or learning styles in your class.

FOR EXAMPLE

Need to see more? Turn to the Math Cube and Comprehension Cube reproducibles on pages 112 and 113, respectively.

NOW LOOK WHAT YOU'VE DONE!

Within the whole group, you've managed to engage all of your students. You've given kinesthetic learners a chance to move around a bit and work with the cube. You've given auditory learners a chance to respond in ways that are meaningful to them, and you've given visual learners a chance to show what they know by reading and writing. At the same time, you've also incorporated higher-level thinking skills in your teaching.

Are you feeling a bit more at ease about differentiating instruction in a whole-group setting? I hope so. I want you to *open* each window of opportunity—not jump out of it!

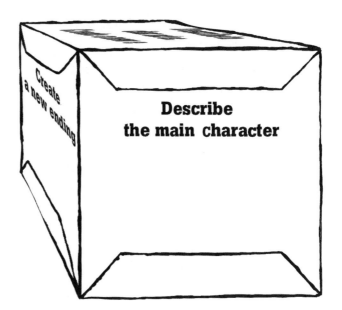

I Have/Who Has?

I Have/Who Has? is a great alternative to work sheets for studying and reviewing content. It's quick, gets students engaged immediately, and can be used in any content area.

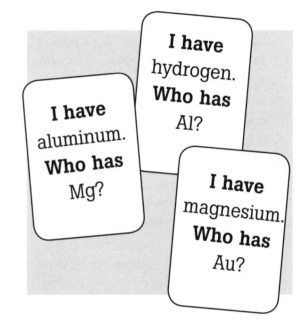

I have aluminum. **Who has Mg?**

I have hydrogen. **Who has Al?**

I have magnesium. **Who has Au?**

CHEW ON IT

For every 10 to 15 minutes of sage-on-the-stage instruction, ask your students to "chew" or process the information in some way. For example, ask students to:

- pair off and discuss with their partners what they've learned.

- participate in a whip—a process of your going around the class and getting quick responses to questions. Just be sure to give your students wait time before you start the whip around.

- play a game such as Wheel of Fortune, Jeopardy, Hollywood Squares, or I have/Who Has?

No matter which of these approaches you use, always "chunk" the information—give students manageable amounts of information at one time—and give them a chance to "chew" on it!

STEP BY STEP

- Turn to the I Have/Who Has? reproducible on page 114. Make enough copies so that each student can get one card.

- Cut the cards apart.

- If you like, laminate the cards so you can reuse them later with different content.

- Fill in the blank spaces so that each card has a question on the bottom and the answer to a different question at the top. Make sure that the question on each card has a corresponding answer on one—and only one—other card.

- Give one card to each student.

- Call on any student to start the game by reading only the question (not the answer) on his card.

- Explain that whoever has the card with the answer to that question should say,

"I have [the answer to the question]" and should then ask, "Who has [the question on his card]?" For example, if I'm the first student to start, I might say, "Who has the 1st Amendment?" The student with the answer would say, "I have freedom of speech. Who has the 19th Amendment [or whatever question is on the card]?"

* Continue until the student who started the game is able to give the answer from his card.

VARIATIONS

Variation 1: I think sometimes it's good to be a little devious. Just think what might happen if you were to "arrange" things so that a particular student received a certain card that would allow him to experience some success. You would be differentiating for the way that student feels about learning and the classroom.

Variation 2: Think of all the possibilities for content you can cover with this strategy. You can work with vocabulary and definitions, math expressions, the Periodic Table, and much more.

NOW LOOK WHAT YOU'VE DONE!

Talk about auditory reinforcement—this strategy has it! It's a great approach for those auditory learners. It also invites all students to be better listeners.

SPEAKING OF LISTENING

Wouldn't you agree that we all could be better listeners? There's a reason each letter in the word "silent" is also in the word "listen." (You're checking me on that right now, aren't you? I can just see you!)

Question-Tac-Toe

AQuestion-Tac-Toe is a menu of questions that can help students think at different levels of Bloom's taxonomy. This strategy also allows you to differentiate assignments over the course of a unit of study. By using a menu like this, you give students a chance to participate in activities or create end products appropriate for their individual learning styles. If you like, assign point values to encourage students to try harder questions.

STEP BY STEP

- Using one of the Question-Tac-Toe reproducibles on pages 115–118, create a menu of possible activities, questions, and/or end products students can respond to. Post the grid on a bulletin board in your classroom or use it as a handout for each student.

- Have the students choose at least three of the questions—perhaps one from each line—to answer over a period of time.

NOW LOOK WHAT YOU'VE DONE!

A Question-Tac-Toe can be a wonderful way to honor individual learning styles and readiness levels. By allowing each student to show what he's learned in a way he chooses, this strategy also builds on student strengths—and therefore fosters self-confidence.

Reproducible

Chapter Two, Strategy #7

Question-Tac-Toe

Knowledge	Comprehension	Application
(Write, List, Define, Label) Write our school mission statement without looking at it.	*(Explain, Compare, Summarize)* In your own words, explain this phrase from our school mission statement: "confident and competent citizens."	*(Apply, Illustrate, Diagram)* What does "confident and competent" mean in our classroom?
Analysis	**Synthesis**	**Evaluation**
(Analyze, Categorize, Solve) What parts of the mission statement refer to you? To our school? Compare our mission statement to the Pledge of Allegiance.	*(Adapt, Compose, Create)* Write a mission statement for our class that you think everyone would support.	*(Judge, Recommend, Forecast)* Should every school be mission driven? Support your position.
Comprehension *(Outline)* Your Choice	**Evaluation** *(Debate)* Your Choice	**Synthesis** *(Compose)* Your Choice

115

Question-Answer Relationships

How often do your students say to you, "But the answer isn't here!"? Help is on the way! The Question-Answer-Relationships (Q.A.R.) strategy improves the questioning skills of teachers and the comprehension and questioning skills of students. Question-Answer Relationships (Raphael, 2006) is a strategy that considers questions not in isolation but in relation to a piece of text and to a student's knowledge base. It's very effective in getting students to go beyond parroting literal, superficial information to actually thinking about it.

The Q.A.R. strategy lets your students know that they must think in more than one way in order to answer questions from a text. When you ask questions in each of the Q.A.R. categories, you expose students to higher levels of thinking. Better yet, when *students* are the ones making up questions in each of those categories, they are generating questions that call for higher levels of thinking.

STEP BY STEP

- There are two major types of Question-Answer Relationships: In-the-Book questions and In-My-Head questions.

- There are two types of In-the-Book questions:

  ✓ With Right-There questions, the answer is found in one place in the text. In *Goldilocks and the Three Bears,* a Right-There question would be, "What did Mama Bear pour into the bowls?"

  ✓ Think, Search, and Find questions go one step further. With these, the answer is found in different places in the text. A Think, Search, and Find question would be, "Where did Goldilocks go inside the bears' house?"

- There are also two types of In-My-Head questions:

  ✓ For Author-and-Me questions, the answer is not found in the text, but the text still has to be read. While reading, the student must look for clues and evidence in the text and then combine those with the student's own background knowledge to figure out the answer. "How did Goldilocks feel when she saw the three bears?" would be an Author-and-Me question.

  ✓ An On-My-Own question is not dependent on the text. Rather the answer comes from the student's prior knowledge. For example: "Have you ever known that someone else had been in your bedroom at home? How did you know?" You have a reason for teaching this last category, even though it relies on prior knowledge and not on the text. If you don't teach students the different types of questions, then they sometimes tend to answer everything as if it were an On-My-Own question. Teach this category so you can point out these things to students.

- Copy the Question-Answer Relationships and Q.A.R. Questions reproducibles from pages 119–123, using the enlarging feature on the copier to make the copies as big as possible. Laminate these posters and then hang them in your classroom.

- Teach the Q.A.R. strategy with a variety of reading selections. Cartoon strips and children's picture books are great for introducing older students to this approach because with these books the students don't get bogged down in the content while learning the strategy.

- Once you're sure students understand the four types of questions, have them begin to generate their own questions in the Q.A.R. format.

WHY IT MATTERS

The Q.A.R. strategy is a good system for evaluating both the types of questions you're asking students and the types of questions they're generating. Neither you nor the students want to rely solely on the Right-There or Think, Search, and Find questions. The questions that call for higher-level thinking are usually the Author-and-Me questions. The terms "Right There," "Think, Search, and Find," "Author and Me," and "On My Own" are a nice working vocabulary for you and your students.

- Hold all students accountable for making up each of the types of questions, but tier or level the activity according to readiness or reading level. Those students below grade level might use children's picture books to make up their questions, the on-grade-level students could use on-grade-level texts to make up their questions, and the above-grade-level students could use graphs or charts or some type of non-standard text to generate their questions.

NOW LOOK WHAT YOU'VE DONE!

Once students are familiar with this strategy, when someone comes to you and says, "But the answer's not here!" you can reply, "Maybe that's not a Right-There question!"

FOR EXAMPLE

Sample text like this, which will engage the sports fans in your class, provides a great way to introduce the Q.A.R. strategy.

Baseball players and their fans are always interested in batting averages. Batting averages are used to measure the hitting performance of the players. To figure a batting average, you divide the number of hits a player has by the batter's official at bats. An official at bat does not include the number of times the batter has hit a sacrifice fly, walked, or been hit by a pitch. So if a player has 10 hits and 50 official at bats, the batting average would be calculated as follows: 10 divided by 50 is equal to .200. Batting averages are always recorded as three-digit decimals.

Another reason batting averages are important is that they are used to help determine the hitting order of the team. A batting average of .300 or above is considered very good in major league baseball.

Batting averages are frequently reported in chart form, like this:

This Season	At Bats	Singles	Doubles	Triples	Home Runs	Batting Average
Player A	400	65	25	3	4	.240
Player B	397	70	30	2	9	.280
Player C	395	75	36	6	11	.320

Once students have read the text and chart, pose these questions:

Right There: How is a batting average calculated? (The answer is in one place in the text.)

Think, Search, and Find: How are batting averages used? (The answer is in several places in the text.)

Author and Me: How much higher is Player C's batting average than Player A's? (This question is text dependent. The student must read the text/chart, looking for clues and evidence in the form of the numbers on the chart. He then must combine that information with what's "in his head"—the process of subtraction—to figure out the answer.)

On My Own: Are you a baseball fan? (The answer to this question does not depend on the text.)

D.E.A.Q.

Key words and sample questions can encourage both you and your students to generate questions that address a wide range of thinking skills. D.E.A.Q. stands for Drop Everything And Question. It encourages students to take responsibility for their learning.

STEP BY STEP

- Turn to the reproducibles for Key Words & Sample Questions from Bloom's Taxonomy on pages 105–106. Make one copy of those pages for each student in the class.

- Hand out those copies to the students and assign different levels of questions to individuals or groups of students. Explain that the students' task is to come up with a written set of questions that are at the assigned level and relate to a specific topic of study.

- Set a timer for 5–10 minutes and challenge students to see how many questions they can generate in that time.

- That includes you! Do the same thing the students are doing at the same time they're doing it. I'd suggest that you assign yourself one of the higher levels.

- Collect all the questions. Look through what you've collected and choose appropriate questions to include in class discussions, on assessments, as journal topics, or as subjects for group discussions. Of course, include some of your own questions in the mix.

FOR EXAMPLE

Math: Imagine a world with no circles, triangles, or parabolas. Write two paragraphs about what life would be like. (synthesis)

Science: List all the ways you can think of in which matter and energy interact. (knowledge)

Social studies: Explain the effect of the assassination of President John Kennedy on the people of the United States. (comprehension)

Literacy: Compare and contrast two novels. Consider characters, settings, conflicts, themes, tone, literary devices, symbols, and so on. (analysis)

NOW LOOK WHAT YOU'VE DONE!

You've differentiated the level of questions you assigned certain students according to their readiness for the content. By directing the more in-depth and challenging question assignments to the students who were ready for that kind of complexity and asking other students to generate those questions that simplify the content, you've helped everyone to succeed. You can apply this same kind of differentiation (readiness for content) when you ask individuals or groups of students to *respond* to questions the class has generated.

T.H.I.N.K.

If you want a fun and exciting questioning tool, include T.H.I.N.K. questions in your daily teaching. T.H.I.N.K. stands for Thoughts, How Come, What If, Name and Next, Kind of Alike and Kind of Different. Remember that in a differentiated classroom, you want to challenge all students to think creatively and at higher levels. Involving all students in answering these questions will help you do that. What may differ is how you *get* each student to the higher levels. In some cases, you may want to offer extra credit for answering some of these questions.

STEP BY STEP

- Pose a question from each of the T.H.I.N.K. categories once a day. The box on this page has some examples to get you started; you'll find more in the reproducibles on pages 124–127.

- Use these questions for warm-up activities, for transition times (e.g., those last few moments at the end of a class period), and as anchor activities (assignments that the rest of the class works on when you need to give your attention to a smaller group of students).

- You can further differentiate this strategy by having some of the more academically able students make up their own T.H.I.N.K. questions. Or you can challenge those students by combining some

FOR EXAMPLE

T is for Thoughts/Feelings/Opinion/Point-of-View Questions: "In your opinion, should junk food be banned from vending machines?"

H is for How-Come Questions: "How come car insurance is higher for young people than for adults?"

I is for What-If Questions: "What if your mom had your dad's job and your dad had your mom's job?"

N is for both Name and Next Questions: "Name all the ways erosion can affect landforms." "Global oil demand exceeds supply. What do we do next?"

K is for Kind-of-Alike and Kind-of-Different Questions: "How is radioactive isotope half life similar to population doubling? How is treaty ratification in the Senate different from Supreme Court Justice confirmation?"

T.H.I.N.K. questions. For example, you might say, "How has the move toward a capitalist economy differed in China and post-Soviet Russia and which has been more effective?" (That would be a combination of a Kind-of-Alike/Kind-of-Different Question with a Thought/Opinion Question.)

NOW LOOK WHAT YOU'VE DONE!

T.H.I.N.K. questions will bring out positive emotions in all of your students. And you'll be surprised at the insightful responses and the higher-level thinking you'll get.

Talk with F.R.E.D.

Have you ever noticed that it's often hard to question your students in a whole-group setting in a way that will really guide them through the steps of critical thinking? What you need is a cheat sheet—and that's exactly what this strategy gives you. Talk with F.R.E.D. is a structured way to take your students to the highest levels of thinking. F.R.E.D. stands for <u>F</u>acts, <u>R</u>eflections, <u>E</u>valuation, and <u>D</u>ecisions.

STEP BY STEP

- Before students read a text, watch a presentation or video, or participate in an event, write a list of questions that you want to ask the class. Base your questions on the Talk with F.R.E.D. guidelines. (See the Talk with F.R.E.D. reproducible on page 128.) Concentrate on open-ended questions that your students can't answer with "yes" or "no." Be sure to tailor the questions to the subject and to the group of students.

- After the class reads the text or is otherwise introduced to new content, ask your questions. Following the Talk with F.R.E.D. format will help you get students engaged and will stimulate a meaningful discussion.

INTRODUCING F.R.E.D.

Facts: These are questions that get at what your students have seen, heard, or experienced in other ways.

Reflections: These are questions that get your students' emotions involved by finding out how they feel.

Evaluation: These questions invite your students to make meaning.

Decisions: These questions help students with decisions or resolves.

FACTS
- What scenes or images do you remember?
- What bits of conversation do you remember?
- What facts do you remember?
- What other things did you observe?
- What facts do you know about _____?

REFLECTIONS
- What was your first response to the scenes, etc.?
- Were you excited? Curious? Nervous?
- How did you feel when you watched the video or read the text?

EVALUATION
- What were the most significant events?
- Was this book or video important to you? Why or why not?
- What was your greatest insight, or what was the biggest thing you learned?
- What was the most interesting part for you? Why?

DECISIONS
- What would you say about this text or video to someone who's not here?
- What decisions would you make now that you've read this text or watched this video?
- Would you recommend this to another student? Why or why not?

- Spend three to four minutes at each step of questioning.

- Ask students to elaborate on their answers by giving some specific examples.

- This strategy is also useful with small groups and with individual students. For example, try meeting one-on-one with a struggling student and using this strategy to get her to broaden her perspective, gain insight, and make a better plan. In that case, you might ask:

  ✓ **Facts:** What are your grades? What is your study routine? Why do you suppose you're struggling?

  ✓ **Reflections:** How do you feel about your grades?

  ✓ **Evaluation:** What does it mean if you fail a subject? What impact could failing have on your goals?

  ✓ **Decisions:** What plan can you make to reverse this situation?

NOW LOOK WHAT YOU'VE DONE!

One of the traits you can differentiate for is how your students feel about the learning experience. You can use this strategy to communicate to students that you care, but you can also use it to show that in the classroom, the responsibility for learning is shared. Shared responsibility means that students set learning goals and become active, contributing members of the class—not just passive observers marking time until the bell rings for the end of the period.

MODELING TIPS

Before turning students loose to work in groups or on an assignment, think through the process or assignment aloud. You might say to students, "The last sentence in the first paragraph confused me, so I marked it with a sticky note. Later, my confusion was cleared up. So a strategy for me is to keep reading when I am confused because often the author will clear up the confusion."

Model directions for students, too. You can show them exactly what it is they're to do either by demonstrating it yourself or by having other students model the process.

Planning Questions Are the Key

The key to successful differentiation is knowing your individual students. You need to know each student's readiness, how he learns best, what interests him, and what he thinks and feels about the classroom. If you know those things, you can help students succeed in your whole-group setting by proactively planning when, how, and for which students you need to differentiate.

Does this mean you do this all the time, 24 hours a day, with every unit, every class, and every student? No. But it does mean that you are conscious of what will work and what won't work for each student.

STEP BY STEP

- We've talked about how you can differentiate when you question your students. Now let's take a look at questions you can ask *yourself* as you plan your instruction that will help you to differentiate in your classes.

- Consider the content or the "what" of your teaching and how your students will access that content. Ask yourself:

   ✓ What are the standards I'm addressing and assessing in this content?

   ✓ What are the concepts and skills to be mastered?

   ✓ Is there a guiding question or questions that might shape the study of this content?

   ✓ How can I make this content relevant to my students?

   ✓ How will I figure out what the students already know? What will I do with that data? How can I help them build on prior experiences?

   ✓ What would be appropriate and meaningful ways for students to gain access to this content? How can I engage the students and not just lecture the majority of the time? (Possibilities might include Internet research, field trips, simulations, and guest speakers.)

- Think about the process or the activities the students will engage in to make meaning of the content. Ask yourself these questions:

   ✓ When students are involved in an activity, will it lead to their mastery of the content?

   ✓ Are the activities in which students will be involved related to the guiding questions and the curricular goals of this unit of study? (This is important. If you don't think about this, you might find you're planning activities that aren't related to the goals of the unit of study.)

   ✓ Will the activities I've planned for this unit of study challenge the students appropriately and require them to think critically about the content?

✓ Are the activities engaging and meaningful to students?

✓ Are the activities age appropriate?

✓ Am I using multiple resources to teach this content?

✓ Do the materials and activities I'm using address a wide range of reading levels and learning profiles, and do they reflect the particular interests of my students in this class?

✓ Am I building in some choices for students in terms of how they work and what activities they engage in?

• Move on to the product or the ways your students will show you what they've learned. Ask yourself these questions:

✓ How will my students show that they've mastered the content?

✓ Will the ways my students show that they've mastered the content involve higher levels of thinking as well as in-depth understanding?

✓ Will the products my students develop encourage them to integrate and apply what they've learned?

✓ Could I work with all my students to establish class criteria for success with products?

✓ Could I work with individual students to help each add his own personal criteria?

✓ Could my students have choices as to how they'll express their learning?

• Take a look at the learning environment of your classroom. Ask yourself these questions in the context of each class you teach:

✓ Have I talked with my students about the fact that we all learn differently?

✓ Are my students aware of classroom agreements, responsibilities, and procedures so that our learning together will proceed smoothly?

✓ Do my plans show that I'm appropriately challenging each of my students, making sure that they can all be successful in a safe and caring learning environment?

FOR EXAMPLE

Let's say you're teaching ninth-grade earth science, and you know that some of your students (visual/spatial types) really love to draw. Ask those students to draw the parts of glacial terrain (arêtes, moraines, tarns, and so on). Ask the students who seem more "active" (those bodily/kinesthetic types) to act out the process of glacial movement and the effects it has on geological features. Ask those students who excel in language arts (verbal/linguistic types) to write a report on the process of glaciation.

NOW LOOK WHAT YOU'VE DONE!

In a differentiated classroom, you're committed to meeting the needs of all your students. This is a very different mind-set from just operating from the teacher's edition and hoping most of the students "get it." When you make an effort to match lessons with different learning styles, you reach more students and build depth for all students. Even if you just make a point of creating assignments that appeal to a wide range of learning styles and having all students complete those assignments, you're giving more students a chance for success.

Five Questions to Ask

The magic of the reading-writing interaction is that it's all about asking and answering questions. Good readers continually ask questions while reading. Poor readers and those trying only to "make it through" the material tend to merely move their eyes across the page. The Five Questions to Ask graphic organizer helps students remember five critical questions to ask while reading. This strategy invites readers to stay focused, engaged, and thinking as they read.

STEP BY STEP

- Make one copy of the Five Questions to Ask reproducible on page 129 for each student in the class—but don't distribute them yet.
- Write on the board the five questions from that organizer.
- Read to your students a newspaper editorial, a passage from a novel, or a selection from a textbook. As you read, stop periodically and model for students how to use the five questions with their own reading.
- Once you're comfortable that students understand how to respond to the questions, give each student his copy of the Five Questions to Ask graphic organizer. Ask students to use the organizer when they get "stuck" with their independent reading. Explain that at those times, each

THE FIVE QUESTIONS

1. **Visualization:** What mental pictures do I see?
2. **Connections:** What does this remind me of?
3. **Inference:** What do I know now, even though I wasn't told the information in the text?
4. **Prediction:** What might happen next?
5. **Summarization/Conclusions:** What was this mostly about?

student should write her answers to the questions in the blank spaces of the organizer. If she needs more room, she can use a separate sheet of paper.

NOW LOOK WHAT YOU'VE DONE!

You've differentiated for struggling or inattentive readers by giving them an organizer to support their self-questioning as they read. This is a way to help them with comprehension all across the curriculum.

Now It's Your Turn to Reflect on This Chapter

What is your "aha!" or insight or thinking after reading this chapter?

_____

_____

_____

_____

What strategy will you try first? How will you use it in your classroom?

_____

_____

_____

_____

How and why might you tailor one of the strategies in this chapter to meet the needs of a specific student or students?

_____

_____

_____

_____

Flexible Grouping Window

I bet you're thinking that this title really sounds crazy! How can you possibly have grouping if you have a whole group?

It all changes when you add the word "flexible."

When I went to school, the standard approach was that everyone sat in rows in classrooms most of the day. We had little or no "legal" interaction with our classmates (we had plenty of "illegal" interaction whenever

A MANAGEMENT TIP

Be sure you have specific procedures so students know how they can get help when you're working with a small group of students. For example, you might establish the rule of "Ask Three Before Me." Anyone with a question must ask three other students before coming to you.

the teacher wasn't watching) and very little variety of groupings. We listened to lectures in most of our classes. I would label this type of grouping as fixed and not flexible.

Now fast forward to today's secondary-school classrooms. In many cases, you'll find that same familiar pattern. Maybe one of those classrooms is yours. I'm sure your heart is in the right place; you want all of your students to be successful. But you might have relatively small blocks of time and large classes of students with varied backgrounds and skills. Some might be ready for an in-depth study of the theme of a novel, some might struggle to make it through the novel, and a few won't even read it. (The students in that last group are the ones who have learned to fake read and fake listen most of the time.)

You think teaching to their individual needs sounds great. But that clock on the classroom wall is ticking, and you have a lot of content to cover. Whole-class instruction usually requires less preparation time than a less traditional approach. So to get everything in, you usually resort to the familiar method of whole-class instruction for the block of time you have.

This chapter will demonstrate that you do have another option: flexible grouping. Flexible grouping is the practice of grouping students according to their learning needs and the goals of a particular lesson. This is not the same kind of grouping we had when I went to school; in those days, we had groups, but they were set in stone. Once you were in a group, for the most part that was the group you stayed in.

Flexible groups are set in Jell-O.

They're for the short term. Once each individual learner's needs and learning goals are met, the groups dissolve—just like the Jell-O. Just as you don't make Jell-O every day, you don't necessarily use flexible grouping every day. Groups are formed and re-formed as appropriate for particular activities.

For example, one day you might start out in the whole group to watch a video, then break up into smaller, differentiated groups for the follow-up, and finally return to the whole group to share the products from the smaller groups. The fluid and flexible groups that are created could last five minutes or they could last a whole class period. It all depends on the needs of the learners and the objectives of the lesson.

You're probably freaking out right now, thinking, "Wait a minute! I bought this book thinking it was going to show me how to differentiate instruction totally in a whole-group setting!" Don't freak out. You're not giving up on teaching students in a whole-group situation. You're going to vary the grouping patterns at certain times—not every day. Think of

it as having subdivisions within your whole group. Rest assured: you can do this!

TYPES OF GROUPS

What are some of the groupings that could occur in your whole-group setting? Let's take a look at a few possibilities:

- **Whole group:** Clearly, this is one way to group students. The whole-group approach can often be the most effective choice when you're introducing new concepts, leading a discussion, facilitating a class debate, demonstrating how to do something, giving directions, or getting students involved in a team-building activity.

- **Small groups of varying degrees of readiness (heterogeneous):** This type of grouping works well when students are

involved in cooperative learning activities, when they need to learn from one another, or when the goal is building social and collaborative skills.

- **Small groups of like readiness (homogeneous):** This type of grouping works well when the goal is for students who have similar levels of readiness in a skill or subject to work together.

- **Independent or individual work:** You are used to this grouping arrangement. When your students are being assessed for mastery of content or when they're practicing a skill, this is the grouping you probably use. Individualizing can also be used for contracts, projects, etc.

GENERAL GROUPING GUIDELINES

That's the theory—but you want to know how to actually do this in your classes. Let's talk about practicalities. And let's start with some general grouping guidelines.

I'd suggest that you begin by assessing your current grouping practices. Consider a week's time and reflect on what percentage of the time in all your classes is devoted to whole-group instruction, what percentage to small-group instruction, and what percentage to individual students working independently. The percentages must add up to 100 percent.

One way to think about flexible grouping in your whole-group setting might be to think about having the whole class together at the beginning of a lesson. This is good for initiating activities and building a sense of community. During a lesson, students might work in a variety of groupings as they make sense of the content at different rates and at varied levels of complexity.

Maybe you want your class to read the same text, but your students require varying levels of support. In that case, you might take those students for whom the reading won't be difficult and have them read either independently or with a small group. You might need to read with those students for whom it will be difficult to read the text independently. Still others—those who are primarily auditory learners—might prefer to listen to a recorded version of the text if that's available. At the conclusion of a lesson, you'd have your class come together again to discuss what they've

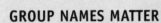

GROUP NAMES MATTER

I've found that it helps, when grouping students by their readiness for content, to name the groups in a way that reflects the content being taught: the "Supply and Demand Club," "Club Federal Reserve," or "Team Sigmund Freud." Refer to groups, clubs, work teams, clinics, pairs, triads, or quads. You know what names will work best with your students. Quirkiness is fine. Don't hesitate to have fun with this and to present it with a sense of humor.

When I was in school—and you may be able to relate to this—the common practice was to have three set groups. Especially in the younger grades, those groups often were called something like the "Robins," "Bluebirds," and "Buzzards." The groupings never changed; once you were a Buzzard, you stayed a Buzzard. And if you're a Buzzard forever, what's going on is really tracking; students are just staying in the same groups day after day and, in some cases, year after year.

learned and identify further questions or topics for future study.

How do you make the groups in your classroom more flexible and fluid? In the beginning, it may take a conscious effort on your part to avoid always grouping by your students' readiness for certain content. But you can do it!

Consider grouping by what students are interested in or how they learn. For example, during a unit on probability, students might start out in readiness groups according to what they already know about probability. Then, at a later point in this unit, you might give students a choice of working on probability involving number cubes or (if your state allows) gambling. Grouping by students' interests changes the student groupings so that individuals are never identified with a single skill or readiness group throughout an entire unit of study.

GROUP SIZE

You'll also need to make some decisions about group size. Options you might want to use at different times include the following:

- **Pairs:** Pairing can maximize participation and achievement if sharing between the two students is timed (see the Timed-Pair Paraphrase strategy on page 19).

- **Triads or quads:** These add more ideas to be considered. They also give you options for creating groups that are more diverse in terms of learning profiles, interests, and social skills. For example, you could have three students with different learning profiles work together to create an "expanded" definition of a vocabulary term or concept. Let's say the term is *photosynthesis*. The visual/spatial student might draw a picture of the process, the bodily/kinesthetic student might

act it out, and the musical student might create a rap about it.

- **Groups of five:** Have you ever heard the expression, "In groups of five, students can hide"? To prevent this, if you use groups of five or more, it's important to structure participation. (See the Numbered Heads Together strategy on page 70 as an example of structured group participation.)

BUILDING IN ACCOUNTABILITY FOR GROUP WORK

Group work in your classroom will be successful only if you set it up to include both group and individual accountability. Group accountability means that the success of the group depends on the success of all members of the group; students must have an underlying commitment to the effort and success of the group. Individual accountability means that the success of the individual members is independent of the success or failure of others.

SAMPLE GROUP ROLES

This is a basic list. You and your class may want to add other possibilities.

Leader: Keeps group going; facilitates group work

Timekeeper: Monitors the time

Materials manager: Gets all necessary materials for the group

Recorder: Pulls together or summarizes in writing the work of the group

Reporter: Summarizes the work of the group orally for the rest of the class

Encourager: Encourages each member to do his best work

Here are some of the ways you can incorporate both individual and group accountability in your classroom:

- Have each group complete an evaluation of how well the group functioned. (See the reproducible for How Well Did We Work Together? on page 130.)

- Before breaking students into groups, explain why you're doing group work or partner work. Reasons might include building social skills, improving listening and communication skills, encouraging students to be constructive, and giving them opportunities to voice their opinions and to back up those opinions. Working toward all of these goals leads to higher achievement for all students.

- Have each group develop working agreements or norms (see the Group Norms reproducible on page 131), as well as a list of roles and responsibilities of each group member.

- Discuss with students issues such as what to do or say to a group member who is not choosing to do her part, or ways to become more tolerant of the student who

FOR EXAMPLE

In the case of a group member who is choosing not to do his part, a member might say, "It takes all of us working together to do this. Can I help you to keep us all on the right track?" Or in the case of the group member who wants to overachieve, someone might make a statement such as "You're really helping us meet our group goal. Each of us needs to have a part in this. Could you watch and help each member as we work toward our goal?"

What's important is for students to understand what it means to encourage one another. It helps to brainstorm and role play ways to convey that encouragement.

wants to overachieve. Class time is well spent when you and your class decide on comments that encourage one another.

You also need to plan for individual accountability. Here are some ways to do *that*:

- Have each group member complete an individual task that you can assess.

- Weight the final grades so that the individual assessments are worth more than the group work. For example, you might decide that individual work is worth 80 percent of a grade and group work is worth 20 percent. In this way, you won't be punishing those students who do their personal best for the performance of someone who did not participate fully in the group effort.

YOUR ROLE: COACH AND FACILITATOR

As you begin your journey into more flexible approaches to grouping, think of yourself as both a coach and a facilitator of learning in your classroom. At times, some students might need to attend a "coaching clinic" with you for some instructional support. Maybe your class is working on developing ideas in their writing. You notice that a few students seem to need some additional strategies for elaborating on their ideas. You invite those students to a "coaching clinic," in which you provide them with additional strategies.

At other times your role might be to act as the facilitator of the various groups working in your room. As a facilitator of learning, your job at those times is to support all students in doing their best work and their best thinking. You might tell students the focus of a unit of study and then ask them their particular areas of interest within that broad focus. Students could then work with like-interest groups to explore the content.

Another time, you might offer students a menu of choices for approaching a particular assignment and then conference with them to help them with their choices. This behavior is very different from the continual sage-on-the-stage approach to instruction.

WHAT DOES THIS HAVE TO DO WITH DIFFERENTIATING INSTRUCTION ANYWAY?

An old story has it that a father once told his son that he was very proud of the child for being at the top of his class. The son replied, "It really doesn't matter. They teach us the same thing at both ends!"

Flexible grouping is at the heart of differentiating instruction. It's difficult, if not impossible, to really meet the needs of each of your students without using a variety of grouping patterns in your classroom. Varying the grouping allows you to teach to your students' strengths by considering intelligences, skills, readiness, and interests as you establish each group. To put it another way: Do you want to increase student achievement? Vary the grouping structures within whatever time block you have.

Variety is the key. Any decisions that you make about using flexible groups will, of course, be driven by student needs and the objectives of the lesson. Any grouping strategy, however, can be overused. When you vary the grouping patterns you're not only giving yourself a chance to observe your students in a variety of contexts, but you're also helping your students to see themselves and each other in ways that expand—rather than limit—their views of the content and of one another.

One issue that always surfaces when you begin using flexible groupings in your whole-class setting is "What do the rest of the students do if I need to meet with a small group of students?" In the language of differentiation, the term that is used to answer that question is "anchoring."

Anchor activities are things that students can work on during a class period, unit of study, grading period, or longer. Anchor activities need to be related to content, meaningful, and challenging to students—and they need to be things for which students are held accountable. Anchor activities are not the same as what we used to call "seat work," which often was just busywork.

In this chapter, you'll find practical strategies that lend themselves to the variety of grouping options discussed above. And since flexible grouping often means planning meaningful strategies for students who are not part of a group at a particular time, I'm including suggestions for anchor activities as well.

Fair & Equal Are Not the Same

In a differentiated classroom it's important for students to understand that fairness means everyone will get what he needs to be successful. Different groups will often be working on different tasks, so students, as well as parents, need to realize that you have high expectations for everyone in the classroom. They need to know you're not changing the standards everyone must meet, but you're being very deliberate about making the curriculum accessible to each student.

TAKE YOUR CHOICE

You have several options for getting this point across from the beginning. Only you know which of these approaches is likely to work best with each of your classes.

- **Journal prompts:** Ask students to reflect on and write in their journals about their experiences around the issue of fairness. They're likely to have plenty of thoughts on the fairness (or unfairness) of teachers, parents, sports officials, town officials, and others.

- **Concept map:** Work with students to develop a concept map of fairness. (See the Concept Map reproducible on page 132.)

- **Project designs:** Challenge groups of students to design projects in which each member of the group participates in a way that's fair to all. Maybe each member could use her particular strengths to assume responsibility for a different part of the project. Some students in each group might choose to write reports while others might want to be in charge of presenting the reports to the class.

- **Literature:** Find stories or passages in literature that describe examples of fairness. Several scenes in Harper Lee's *To Kill a Mockingbird* are appropriate for this. Try the one in which Scout Finch gets in a fight with her cousin Francis and her uncle tries to lecture her on appropriate language.

NOW LOOK WHAT YOU'VE DONE!

By using any of these strategies with your students before you start differentiating, you make sure that students (and parents!) understand the basic concept of differentiated instruction. Better yet, by participating in any of these activities, students have already had a little taste of what it's all about.

Brainstorming A–Z

This is a very simple strategy that can be used in a variety of ways in a whole-group setting. Try this approach to get students to link what they think they know to what they are about to learn, to invite active listening, and to review content.

TAKE YOUR CHOICE

Give each individual or pair of students a copy of the Brainstorming A–Z reproducible on page 133. Then try any of these ideas:

- **Make a list:** Ask each individual or pair to write down, for each letter of the alphabet, a word that's related to the topic of study. For example, when beginning a unit on geometry, students might write "angle" for A, "circle" for C, etc.).

- **Invite active listening:** Before reading a selection aloud to the entire class, talk with the students about the topic, and then ask them to generate a list. The list should include all the words they can think of that might appear in the text to be read and that begin with a specific letter on the Brainstorming A–Z sheet. For example, if you are reading an article about the problems of childhood obesity, ask your students to brainstorm all the words that start with C and might be included in the article. Students might list words such as "calorie," "candy," and "carbohydrates."

- **Review content:** After studying a topic, have students work in pairs. Ask each

person to use the reproducible as a framework to list all the words she can think of that are related to the topic, describe a character, and so on.

NOW LOOK WHAT YOU'VE DONE!

You can use this strategy as an assessment tool and differentiate your instruction according to the results. You might analyze what the students have been able to complete on the reproducible and then use that data to form readiness groups for instruction. Those students whose answers indicate they don't know much about the topic will need some direct instruction; students who appear to know quite a bit about the topic already might benefit from a more in-depth project related to the content.

You might also want to vary the levels of questions you ask, based on what you've learned in this assessment. Some students might brainstorm basic geometry terms while more advanced students might be challenged to brainstorm all the places outside of school where they might see geometric theorems played out in the real world.

Chapter Three, Strategy #2

Reproducible **Brainstorming A–Z**

NAME: Michael
SUBJECT: geometry

A angle	N
B	O oval
C circle	P prism
D dodecahedron	Q
E	R rectangle
F	S square
G	T triangle
H hexagon	U
I	V
J	W
K	X
L line	Y
M	Z

133

Jigsaw

Jigsaw is a cooperative learning structure (Aronson 1978; Slavin 1994; Kagan 1994, 1998) that can be used in any content area and with any grade level. It helps students to explore material in a relatively short amount of time, and it also builds in both individual and group accountability.

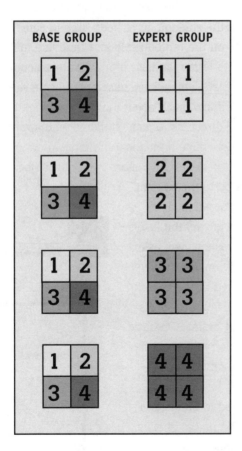

STEP BY STEP

- Have students break into base groups of four students.

- Ask the students in each group to count off.

- Have the number 4 students meet with other number 4s, number 3s meet with other number 3s, 2s with other 2s, and 1s with 1s to form expert groups.

- The job of each expert group is to study a particular area of the content together and then individually meet back with their base groups to teach that content to the base groups. Let's say students are studying the American home front during World War I. You'd assign each expert group a particular topic—maybe one would study the War Industries Board and others would study the Food Administration, women and the war, and the relationship between the war and the flu epidemic of 1918. After the expert group on the War Industries Board meets together, the members return to their base groups to teach the other students about the board's purpose, its specific activities, and the results it produced.

OPTIONS

You can differentiate this strategy in a couple of different ways:

Level of readiness for the content:

If you have a unit of study on Theodore Roosevelt after the class has already studied the Spanish-American War, for example, ask the students for whom the content is difficult to review in their expert group what the class already knows about Roosevelt as a member of the Rough Riders in that war. They can create a timeline with illustrations of Roosevelt's career up to his presidency. A second group can focus on his work in conservation; their assignment is to write a letter to an influential member of Congress in support of a particular environmental bill. A third group can write a newspaper article that focuses on Roosevelt's work as a diplomat once he was elected president—a part of his career that is more complex. Ask the fourth expert group to write a eulogy for Roosevelt that covers his life before and during his presidency and also includes information about his work as a leader of the Progressive party and his efforts to reform the meat-packing industry. When students return to their base groups, each student can share with the others what was done in his expert group.

End products: Let students choose, based on their learning preferences or intelligences, how they'll show you what they've done. When studying westward expansion, for example, expert groups can research the roles of different groups that moved to the western frontier between 1840 and 1900—say, Mormons, Chinese immigrants and Chinese-Americans, Forty-Niners and gold miners, and African-Americans or "Exodusters." The students studying the Mormons might brainstorm ideas together, and then each individual student in that group might draw a cartoon strip illustrating a particular issue faced by Mormons at that time. Or each could make a flowchart on poster board showing why the Mormons moved. Each student would then use his cartoon or flowchart to teach his base group about what he's learned.

NOW LOOK WHAT YOU'VE DONE!

This activity has all sorts of benefits in terms of differentiated instruction. If you require a student to turn in a report, you're allowing for individual assessment. If you require each *group* to turn in a report or take a quiz on the material, you establish group accountability.

The process fosters shared responsibility for learning. And when the students return to their base groups, those students for whom the content is a challenge will not only have the chance to participate in the group discussion but will also benefit from the dialogue with the more advanced learners in the group.

Numbered Heads Together

Like the Jigsaw strategy, Numbered Heads Together is appropriate for multiple content areas and grade levels. It's also a great way to review because it holds each group member accountable for the learning (Kagan 1994, 1998).

STEP BY STEP

- Divide students into groups of four.

- Have students count off in each group so that every group has a number 1, number 2, number 3, and number 4.

- Pose a question or raise an issue for discussion. Have group members put their heads together and brainstorm answers to the question or issue you've posed. Explain that they should discuss the possibilities and come to an agreement. Be sure to give very specific directions for this step. Say something like, "Put your heads together and make sure everybody in your group knows how the Presidential, Congressional, and Judicial offices are filled and can give evidence to support the answer."

- Give the groups time to work together to formulate their responses and to make sure that each group member will be able to respond successfully if called upon.

- Call out a number; within each group, the student with that number should stand.

- Use a spinner or multi-sided gaming die to pick a number; call out that number. Let's say it's 4.

- The number 4 student from every group stands.

- You call on any of those standing to respond, or ask for a choral response if that's appropriate.

NOW LOOK WHAT YOU'VE DONE!

You have both "hogs" and "logs" (some people call them "drivers" and "hitchhikers") in your classroom, and this cooperative learning structure can meet the learning needs of both groups. The "hog" is given the opportunity to teach others in the group, but the "log" can't check out of the activity and go to space camp because she never knows when her number will be called. And the "log" should be successful in responding because you've told the students to make sure everyone knows the group's answer.

Discussion Roles for a Lecture or Video

After students have listened to the same lecture or watched the same video, divide them into groups for active discussions.

STEP BY STEP

• Before class, make enough copies of the Role Cards for a Lecture or Video reproducible on page 134 so that every student in your class can have one card. If there are 24 students in your class, you'll need six copies of the reproducible. Cut the copies into individual cards and laminate them.

• Divide students into heterogeneous groups of four and give each student in each group one of the individual cards from the reproducible.

• Tell students to read what their roles will be for the group discussions. For example, one student might have the role of discussing something she agreed with in the video or lecture.

• Have students watch the video or listen to the lecture.

• Give students time for a group discussion. This is the point at which each member participates based on the role given on his card.

• Give each group a large sheet of bulletin-board paper and some markers.

• Ask each group to figure out a way to show the key elements of its discussion by making a graphic representation on the bulletin-board paper.

* Have each group share its graphic representation with the entire class.

* For example, perhaps a class is watching a video about different religions in the Middle East. After viewing the video, one student would be responsible for summarizing the content of the video, one would be responsible for asking the other group members questions about the video, and so on.

NOW LOOK WHAT YOU'VE DONE!

When they're part of heterogeneous groups and they've been given an assignment before listening to the lecture or watching the video, those students who have trouble concentrating and participating are invited to pay attention as well as to discuss their specific assignments with the others. You're creating a different pathway to help these students become successful.

ROLE-CARD DEFINITIONS FOR USE WITH A LECTURE OR VIDEO

Role	Definition	Examples
Question Asker	Responsible for asking a question of the others in the group about the content of the video or lecture	What are the principle religions represented in the Middle East? What are some of the holy sites of the religions? What are some of the key beliefs of the religions?
Summarizer	Responsible for telling the other students the main points of the video or lecture	The video was about how Islam, Judaism, and Christianity all have historical roots in the Middle East. It was also about how they co-exist with varying degrees of harmony and discord in the different countries there today. It presented some of the key beliefs of each religion as well as some brief history of each.
I agree with . . .	Responsible for discussing those points she agreed with in the video or lecture	I can see some of the common elements of each religion, such as monotheism. I can see why there is so much dispute over certain historical and religious sites in cities like Jerusalem and Bethlehem, and I have a better understanding of the current conflict in southern Lebanon, but I have a hard time grasping how intense religious belief can be. In our community we have several different religious organizations, but they seem to exist with less conflict.
I disagree with or I was surprised by . . .	Responsible for discussing those points he disagreed with or was surprised to learn in the video or lecture	I was surprised by the issues of separation of religion and state in those countries. I didn't realize that there were secularists there, too, and that many of the leaders and populace are not that religious.

Role Cards for Expository Text

This strategy promotes active discussion by using role cards and uses colors to differentiate for different skill levels. The example assumes that you're using blue for the less able and green for the more able students.

STEP BY STEP

- Before class, make one enlarged copy of the Pointer/Signal Words reproducible on page 135 and post it in the classroom for student reference.

- Also make enough copies of the Blue or Green Role Cards for Expository Text reproducibles on pages 136–137 so that every student in your class can have one card that's appropriate for her readiness level. Cut the sheets into individual cards and laminate the cards.

- Divide the students into homogeneous readiness-level groups of four and give each student in each group one of the individual cards from the reproducibles. (Make sure each group has cards for all four roles.)

- Tell students to read their cards to find out what their individual roles will be for the group discussions.

- Have them read the chapter or section of the book.

- Give students time for group discussion. This is the point at which each member participates based on the role on his card.

- Give each group a large sheet of bulletin-board paper and some markers.

- Ask each group to figure out a way to show the key elements of its discussion by making a graphic representation on the bulletin-board paper.

- Have each group share its graphic representation with the entire class.

NOW LOOK WHAT YOU'VE DONE!

You've given students an incentive to participate, and you've differentiated according to abilities.

KEY WORD FINDER
Responsible for identifying key words in the text and being ready to explain to the group what they mean

MAIN IDEA MINDER
Responsible for telling the ma[in idea] of the text

DETAIL PERSON
Responsible for [...]

QUESTION ASKER
Responsible for generating a question about the text that can be answered directly by reading the text

Discussion Cards for Narrative Text

Now you're ready to add one more level of complexity to the role cards. Here's a way to use this approach with narrative text.

STEP BY STEP

- Before class, make enough copies of the Discussion Cards for Narrative Text reproducible on page 138 so that every student in your class can have one discussion card. These do not need to be color coded. Cut the sheets into individual cards and laminate the cards.

- Also ahead of time, write specific discussion questions for students on blue (for less able students) and green (for more able students) strips of paper.

- In class, divide students into groups of four that are homogeneous by readiness level. Give each student in each group one of the individual discussion cards and one or two of the question strips. (Make sure the group has one each of all four discussion cards.) Explain that each student needs to answer the questions on the strips and discuss them with her group, based on the discussion card she's received.

- Have everyone read the book or chapter.

- Give students time for group discussions. This is the point at which each member participates based on the topic given on his card.

SAMPLE BLUE QUESTIONS FOR NARRATIVE TEXT

CHARACTERS

- Who were the main characters? Were they believable?
- Explain how a character in this book reminds you of a character in another book.
- What problems or conflicts did the characters face? How did they overcome them? Or were they overcome by them?

SETTING

- What was the setting? Why do you think the author chose this setting?
- Read to the group a passage that tells something about the setting.
- Can you think of a place that reminds you of this setting or another story you've read that had a setting similar to this one? Give an example.
- Discuss the importance of this particular setting. Why is it crucial that this setting was chosen?

THEME

- What is the theme of the story?
- Have you read another story with a similar theme? Give an example.
- What is a story with a different setting but similar theme? What does this say about the universality of theme?
- How do the themes compare?

RESOLUTION

- What was the problem in this story and how was it solved?

- Give two examples of events that contributed to the problem in the story.

SAMPLE GREEN QUESTIONS FOR NARRATIVE TEXT

CHARACTERS

- Which character would you like to spend a day with and why?

- Think of a situation that involved the main character and discuss how you might have handled it differently.

SETTING

- Think of another setting for the story. How would the story be different if it had taken place in the new setting?

- Why do you think the author chose this setting?

THEME

- How did you learn what the theme was? Give specific examples.

- Give an example of other stories that have the same theme as this one. Did the author of each story use a different technique to present the theme? Give examples.

RESOLUTION

- Can the resolution of this story be transferred to situations in everyday life? Give examples.

- Was the solution to the problem one that you would have selected? Why or why not?

NOW LOOK WHAT YOU'VE DONE!

By assigning different topics, you're teaching to each student's strengths. You're also inviting each student to become engaged in learning because everyone knows she has a specific responsibility.

Think-Tac-Toe

This is a great anchor activity to assign to individual students. It allows them to engage in meaningful work while you're involved with other students in a small group.

STEP BY STEP

- Make a copy of the Think-Tac-Toe reproducible grid on page 139.

Reproducible

Chapter Three, Strategy #8

Think-Tac-Toe

Nutrition Unit

Design a survey to determine class eating habits and make a graph of the findings to share with the class.	Make a poster that compares the nutritional values of various foods. Include portion sizes, calories, fats, and carbohydrates on your poster. Display it for the class.	Create a collage of pictures of healthy foods.
Write a rap or song about what constitutes a healthy diet. Perform it for the class.	Read an article about the importance of good nutrition and write a one-page summary.	Write a letter to the editor of the newspaper about the importance of healthy eating.
Design a PowerPoint presentation on a healthy diet to share with the class.	Collect 10–20 food labels that compare and contrast healthy and unhealthy foods.	Create menus for one week of healthy eating. Be prepared to explain your menus to the class.

139

- Identify nine activities related to content that the class is studying. Make some of the activities more difficult than others.

- Write each activity in one of the squares in the Think-Tac-Toe grid.

- Make one copy of the completed grid for each student.

- Explain to the class that each student is to choose one assignment from each line in order to complete a Think-Tac-Toe. Specify how long they have to finish these assignments.

VARIATIONS

Use any of the reproducibles on pages 140–142 as variations on the Think-Tac-Toe theme.

NOW LOOK WHAT YOU'VE DONE!

You have all sorts of opportunities for differentiating with a Think-Tac-Toe grid. You can give students choices that appeal to different learning styles, different intelligences, or different skill levels. This is exactly what differentiated instruction is all about!

4–6–8

The 4–6–8 chart lets you and your class invest 10 to 15 minutes up front to create a framework that you can use all year long.

STEP BY STEP

• Work with your entire class to construct a 4–6–8 chart that will be posted in the room. If you like, you can start with an enlarged copy of the 4–6–8 reproducible on page 143.

• For the first column, "Characters," work with students to list four different characters from any books they've read. The characters don't all have to be from the same book.

• For the second column, "Settings," work with students to list six different settings where a story could take place.

• For the third column, "Events," work with students to list eight different events that could occur in a story.

• Laminate the completed poster and hang it in the room.

• Circle a character, a setting, and an event, and have the students compose a story using the circled items.

• Each week, change the circled numbers and have the students compose a new story using the circled elements.

VARIATION

Ask certain students to create their own 4–6–8 charts and work from them.

NOW LOOK WHAT YOU'VE DONE!

Once you've prepared the initial chart with the class, you'll find it takes no time at all to prepare each assignment. Just change the circles! In that one initial brainstorming session, you've created 192 possible combinations, and it's likely that virtually every one will allow your students to differentiate themselves according to their individual interests and abilities.

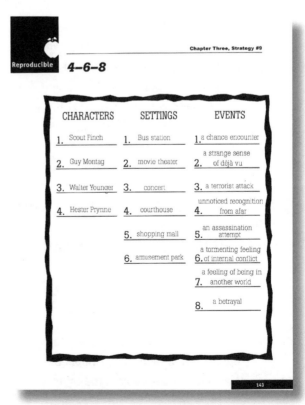

R.A.F.T.

R.A.F.T. is an acronym that stands for Role, Audience, Format, Topic. The R.A.F.T. format asks students to write from a viewpoint other than their own to an audience other than the teacher and in a format other than answering questions at the end of a story or textbook chapter. By incorporating four ingredients of writing and also giving students the opportunity to process and manipulate content, this anchor activity can bring fun and creativity into writing in your classroom.

STEP BY STEP

• Explain to students that this activity requires them to think creatively in response to specific writing prompts.

• Model a sample R.A.F.T. activity. For example, for a unit on health, the assignment might be as follows:

R(OLE)	HEART
A(UDIENCE)	FRENCH FRIES
F(ORMAT)	COMPLAINT
T(OPIC)	EFFECTS OF FAT IN THE DIET

In other words, the heart is to write a letter to the french fries, complaining about the effect on the body of the fat in the fries.

This example will certainly elicit smiles from students, and if you can get middle- or high-school students laughing and thinking, that's quite an accomplishment.

• Write on the board the outline for another R.A.F.T. assignment and ask students to complete it on their own. For a science unit on plants, the R.A.F.T. outline might go like this:

R(OLE)	PLANT
A(UDIENCE)	RAIN
F(ORMAT)	THANK-YOU NOTE
T(OPIC)	RAIN'S ROLE IN GROWTH

• To differentiate, try varying the difficulty of the R.A.F.T. assignments, then asking certain students to complete specific R.A.F.T. activities. Or differentiate by students' interests, letting each student choose the R.A.F.T. exercise she wants to complete.

NOW LOOK WHAT YOU'VE DONE!

You've kept students occupied with meaningful work, got them thinking, enhanced their writing skills, and potentially differentiated according to their interests and skills.

POTENTIAL R.A.F.T. ASSIGNMENTS

R(OLE)	A(UDIENCE)	F(ORMAT)	T(OPIC)
Hyperbola	Asymptote	Love letter	Explain their relationship
Presidential candidate	The public	Candidacy speech	Hope for the future
Unemployed factory worker	Friend	Letter	Looking for work
Reporter	The public	Newspaper article	Causes/effects of the current economic situation
Teacher	Students	Outline or timeline	Events leading to current political/economic/school situation

Now It's Your Turn to Reflect on This Chapter

What is your "aha!" or insight or thinking after reading this chapter?

_____

_____

_____

_____

_____

What strategy will you try first? How will you use it in your classroom?

_____

_____

_____

_____

How and why might you tailor one of the strategies in this chapter to meet the needs of a specific student or students?

_____

_____

_____

_____

Ongoing Assessment Window

For many years of my teaching career, I thought of assessment as the chapter tests, daily quizzes, and homework problems that I routinely gave my students. My students got very used to the routine in our classroom. They got so used to it that all during the week their favorite question was: "Is this going to be on the Friday test?"

My goal was to get everything graded and in the grade book before I left school on Friday afternoons. I would stay until 6 PM if I had to, just so that I could get away from it all for the entire weekend.

Wow! Hasn't the view of assessment changed! When I was in the classroom, standard operating procedure was to teach, teach, teach, and then assess. The students weren't really a part of the whole process. They just waited to see what grades they got on their report cards each quarter.

In later years, as a building principal, I looked at lots of the students' writing papers and tried to give them feedback. However, I struggled there as well. I knew I needed to be specific, but often I would find myself lacking the language that would really help a student grow as a writer.

Luckily, I've learned a few things since then.

WHAT WE KNOW ABOUT ASSESSMENT

We know now that assessment is much more than the weekly tests. We know that ongoing assessment of our students is an essential part of guiding and driving our instruction. We also know that before we assess anything for a final grade, we need to provide many opportunities for students to demonstrate their skills and knowledge in a variety of formats.

And we know more than that. We know assessment works best when we give students an explanation of what's correct and what's incorrect, along with specific suggestions for growth; when we provide that feedback to them in a timely fashion; when we give students an opportunity to continue working on responses until they succeed; and when students are a part of the assessment process. In other words, we get the best results when we make the goals clear and give students the opportunity to assess themselves.

SOME QUICK DEFINITIONS

That much we know. But then things start to get fuzzy. Does your head start to spin when people toss around the terms assessment, evaluation, and grading? Let's establish some definitions. Assessment involves gathering and reviewing data; evaluation is judging the data; and grading is the reporting system.

Think about it for a minute in a different context. Recently a good friend of mine went to the local supermarket because the pharmacy there was offering very inexpensive health screenings. Her blood was drawn and sent away to a lab. She got back a report that listed her total cholesterol, HDL, LDL, ratios, triglycerides, and glucose. She took the report to her doctor, who recommended specific treatment to lower her cholesterol levels.

What happened? The pharmacy staff gathered the data when they drew the blood; that was the assessment. The doctor added to that assessment when he asked my friend questions about her family history and her own health. He evaluated the data when he took all the information and began to judge it. He determined that she had high cholesterol, for which he prescribed a course of treatment. Although he didn't give my friend a formal grade, he did tell her that if he had, she wouldn't have passed his "cholesterol class"!

The doctor's assessment and evaluation, however, led to an intervention (medication) so that my friend wouldn't fail "cholesterol class." The doctor didn't wait until the end to intervene; he was proactive. In our classrooms, our assessment and evaluation must also drive our instruction so that, if necessary, we can intervene to help each student reach success.

A good assessment program in your classroom should include a variety of classroom assessments. You probably already use the traditional assessment vehicles of pop quizzes, teacher-made tests, and tests you get from publishers. I'm not suggesting that you throw those out but rather that you supplement them with some other ways of observing, gathering, and evaluating student work.

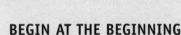

BEGIN AT THE BEGINNING

Turn to pages 144–146 to find reproducibles for the Interests, Intelligences & Ignorances Survey; an Informal Rating Scale to Discover Intelligences; and a Student Learning Contract. The rating scale can help you and your students discover their multiple intelligences; the learning contract is primarily for students who already seem to know the content at a fairly high level. You might want to use the contract if pre-assessments show that a student needs to participate only in parts or maybe none of the whole-group instruction.

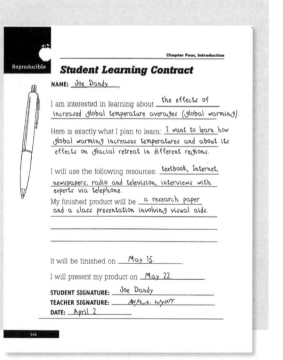

Chapter Four, Introduction

Reproducible

Student Learning Contract

NAME: Joe Dandy

I am interested in learning about the effects of increased global temperature averages (global warming).

Here is exactly what I plan to learn: I want to learn how global warming increases temperatures and about its effects on glacial retreat in different regions.

I will use the following resources: textbook, Internet, newspapers, radio and television, interviews with experts via telephone.

My finished product will be a research paper and a class presentation involving visual aids.

It will be finished on May 15.

I will present my product on May 22.

STUDENT SIGNATURE: Joe Dandy
TEACHER SIGNATURE: Mrs. Wyatt
DATE: April 2

146

WHAT DOES THIS HAVE TO DO WITH DIFFERENTIATING INSTRUCTION ANYWAY?

Ongoing assessment is at the heart of a differentiated classroom. It's very purposeful. It means that your assessment of your individual students' readiness, interests, and ways of learning, as well as your understanding of their thoughts and feelings, is always driving the decisions you make about your instruction. Throughout the learning cycle, you're constantly gathering and reviewing data and making judgments about where your instruction should go—that's how you help students grow and achieve success. Grading is the final step, the one that takes place after instruction is over.

Can ongoing assessment help your students to succeed? You bet!

Of course, ongoing assessment means that you need to be assessing where students are before, during, and after instruction. Each of those phases has its own requirements, so it helps if you think of yourself as an assessor in three areas:

- Pre-assessment: determining students' prior understanding and readiness for content, as well as what interests them concerning the content
- Formative assessment: tracking students' progress throughout the learning process, as well as giving them the opportunity to track their own growth
- Summative assessment: making sure they've reached the goals that have been set

In this chapter you'll find a variety of options for pre-assessment, formative assessment, and summative assessment to use in your whole-group setting. Keep in mind, though, that assessment is only a first step.

WHAT YOU DO WITH THAT DATA IS CRITICAL

Once you've collected it, you need to examine the data and identify the learning differences and similarities in your classroom. Based on what you learn, you need to make decisions about what your instruction will look like. How will you plan instruction for those students who need something different? What about the students who are ready to move on?

In other words, don't bother to pre-assess if you're not going to do something with the data you collect. You wouldn't want your doctor to read the report on your cholesterol levels and say, "Oh, that's not good. Her cholesterol is up to 310. Guess I'd better file that!"

Timing matters, too. Especially in the beginning, you'll need to gather your pre-assessment data early enough so that you can

A MANAGEMENT TIP

Establish a variety of fun and novel ways to select group leaders. You can always have students count off and then use a spinner to select a group leader by number. However, as a change of pace you might want to identify the leader based on any of these attributes:

- Shortest first name or last name
- Tallest or shortest
- Wearing the most red, blue, etc.
- Most brothers, sisters, siblings
- Fewest siblings
- Most recently ate pizza
- Closest birthday
- Lives farthest from the school
- Most colorfully dressed

plan your instruction according to what you learn in your assessments. At times, you may need to adjust your instruction in a couple of ways—for the students who have mastered the content already and for those who will need different types of support to reach that point. Don't let that scare you off. Just make sure you do your assessment early enough so that you leave yourself time to adjust your teaching.

When you get to the formative assessments, timing still matters, but at this point the issue is more one of whether you need to do some reteaching or to adjust the pacing of the instruction—slowing things down or accelerating your teaching. You'll also need to think about *when* you'll gather the additional data from those formative assessments and on which students or groups of students.

A WORD OF CAUTION

Many times teachers will say, "I can't give choices because some tasks are just easier than others or more fun." It's true that sometimes all or most students may choose the same way of demonstrating their learning. My feeling is that that's okay; what you want to do is hold all your students to the criteria you've established.

In other words, students are graded on how well they incorporate what you've asked them to incorporate. You offer lots of ways for students to show you what they've learned, but you give them very specific criteria regarding what they'll be accountable for. In an English class, for example, some students might write essays and some might keep reading journals; others would complete video projects, presentations, or interviews; and still others might show what they've learned through art projects. But all would be responsible for learning the same material. This is a different way of thinking about assessment.

Formative assessment is a big part of differentiating instruction in a whole-group setting, in part because these types of assessments can help you celebrate and honor the diversity in your whole group. As you gather this important data, you'll start to see:

- What entry points into content might be effective for certain students

- How best to group students

- How the students are feeling about their own progress

- How to help students set goals

- What mini-lessons you might need to teach to help all students be successful

This is very different from the teach-teach-teach-test approach!

The more you move toward authentic and performance-based assessment, the more you can differentiate and the more choices you can give your students. Choice motivates students and helps them become partners in the learning that takes place in your classroom.

Human Continuum

Like the four strategies that follow, the Human Continuum is a pre-assessment that lets you find out your students' initial level of knowledge, skills, interests, and attitudes. This information will help you plan your instruction at the most appropriate level for each student.

In addition, your students will be motivated and involved as they become partners in the learning process. They'll gain a better sense of what they already know, as well as a clearer idea of what they need to know. Use this strategy to supplement ones you might already be using—quizzes, questions, observation, etc.—in pre-assessing your students.

STEP BY STEP

- Place labels at the front of your classroom (perhaps along the top of the chalkboard) along a continuum as follows:

    ✓ I know this!

    ✓ I know something about this!

    ✓ I don't know much about this!

- On the floor in front of the cards, make a line with masking tape.

- Ask each student to write on a piece of paper where he would position himself along the continuum to best describe his understanding of the content. (Writing down his self-assessment encourages the student to be honest rather than just following his friends.)

- Once everyone has done that, ask students to stand at the appropriate spot along the masking tape.

- Ask each student to turn to a neighbor and discuss what she knows about the topic and/or why she chose to stand where she did. Or have students share with the whole class.

VARIATION

For an interesting twist, ask students to fold the line in half and then ask each student to share with the person standing opposite him. This means that those who don't know much about the topic end up facing those who think they know quite a bit. You may find that this leads to an interesting discussion!

NOW LOOK WHAT YOU'VE DONE!

With this quick and simple activity, you've already pre-assessed the students, helped them learn how to assess themselves, and developed a basis for differentiating your instruction of this subject.

Five-Finger Reading Gauge

This pre-assessment empowers your students to select reading material at an appropriate level and gets them involved in their own pre-assessment.

MORE TIPS FOR GIVING DIRECTIONS

• Break directions into small chunks. Say, "When I say 'Go,' I want everyone to stand up." Have students do that and then give the next set of directions: "Look around, find someone you haven't worked with this week, and walk to that person." After students are in pairs, give the next set of directions: "Share your thoughts on the character who's the most memorable for you so far." This is better than saying, "Stand up, find a partner, and share your thoughts on your most memorable character."

• Use phrases that invite cooperation from students. Instead of saying "You'll have to work with this group," say, "If you could" or "Would you please work with this group."

• Try color coding directions. Have group 2 follow the directions written in green, group 3 follow the directions written in red, etc.

STEP BY STEP

• Have each student select a book to read and open it to the middle.

• Instruct each student to begin silently reading the page. Add that each time she encounters an unknown word, she should put down a finger.

• Explain that if the thumb or at least one finger is still up at the end of the page, the book is at an appropriate level of difficulty.

NOW LOOK WHAT YOU'VE DONE!

You've given students a do-it-yourself strategy for evaluating the appropriateness of any reading material they choose.

Strategy #3

Handshake or High Five

One of the most powerful things you can do to enhance your instruction is to stand at the door and greet your students by name as they enter the classroom. Greeting them with their choice of a handshake or high five allows you to push that greeting up a notch and get a sense of students' thoughts and feelings before class begins.

STEP BY STEP

- Make a habit of standing in the doorway of your classroom and greeting each student by name as she enters the room.

- Teach students that they may choose how they'd like to be greeted, whether it's with a handshake or a high five.

- Use the same technique as a way to praise students for correct answers or "aha! moments." You might say something like, "Awesome, Mark. Handshake or high five?" Then, based on the student's response, you might slap fives. It's a fun way to interact and show appreciation and recognition, especially once you get to know your students.

- Suppose the student says and does nothing as he enters the room. Then you just say something like, "Good morning, [name]. I'm so glad to see you. How about a high five?"

NOW LOOK WHAT YOU'VE DONE!

By using this method, you can pre-assess your students' thoughts and feelings about class. Those who don't respond may need a minute or two of personalized attention from you. In other words, you can figure out from their reactions which students may be having problems at home or a tough time in an earlier class, so you can give them some extra attention up front and get their focus back on the subject at hand.

Word Toss

This pre-assessment strategy helps students make predictions about text they'll be reading. It also lets you gauge their current knowledge of the content.

STEP BY STEP

- Identify major concepts for the text the students will be reading. Write 7 to 10 words or phrases identifying these concepts on separate pieces of acetate.

- Randomly place the strips of acetate on the overhead so they appear to have been tossed there.

- Ask students to work in pairs or small groups. Explain that each group should write a sentence or two using some or all of the terms on the overhead. The sentences should show how the students predict the terms will be related to each other in the material the class is about to read.

- Have students read their sentences aloud. Don't worry about the accuracy of the statements at this point.

- Have students read the text and check the accuracy of their predictions. Invite them to revise their predictions to reflect what they learned from reading the text.

NOW LOOK WHAT YOU'VE DONE!

By using this strategy, you've given students a chance to practice making predictions and then to go back and evaluate those predictions. You've established prior knowledge. And you've supported reading comprehension by giving the students clues about what they should be watching for in the text.

FOR EXAMPLE

Before reading *A Separate Peace,* by John Knowles, a teacher chose these words for the word toss: "Gene," "Finny," "Elwin 'Leper' Lepellier," "Brinker," "fear," "Olympics," "prized," "enlists." One group of students wrote: "Gene prized the Olympic medal he received after beating Finny." Another group wrote: "Leper enlists in the army and learns to overcome his fear." The students were curious and motivated to see which group got it right. So in a clever way, the teacher had them predict, set purposes, and pre-assess.

Anticipation Guide

This strategy helps students anticipate the direction of the text. At the same time, it gives you a chance to pre-assess their knowledge of the content.

STEP BY STEP

- To prepare an Anticipation Guide, identify the major concepts students will be learning in a particular unit of study.

- Craft three to seven statements around the general theme of the material. These statements should be ones that students can agree or disagree with and that will invite discussion.

- List these statements on a work sheet, make copies of the sheet, and give one copy to each student.

- Instruct students to read each statement and mark whether they agree or disagree with it.

- Accept all answers and invite discussion. This will be the point when you can discover misconceptions or student beliefs that might need some clarification or discussion before studying or reading.

- Read the text or proceed with instruction.

- After they read or study the content, have students review their statements. Give them a chance to change their responses based on what they've read or learned.

NOW LOOK WHAT YOU'VE DONE!

Once again, you've set up students to know what to look for in the content they're about to read or material they're about to study. You've also established an understanding of their prior knowledge of the content.

Anticipation Guide

	Agree	Disagree
War is always bad.	_____	_____
There are many different ways to manage conflict.	_____	_____
Most of the time, war needs to be avoided.	_____	_____

FOR EXAMPLE

Statements for Anticipation Guides could include ones along these lines:

- It's okay to be jealous.

- If you make the wrong choices, you eventually get whatever you deserve.

- Insects are low in fat and make a nutritious snack in some parts of the world.

- The firing of coal in one hemisphere can affect weather patterns and pollution in another.

- Your future is your choice, not a matter of fate.

Signal Cards

This formative assessment strategy, like the two that follow, provides you with options for monitoring student progress and offering feedback during a unit of study. You can also use these strategies to improve and make decisions about your instruction. This approach is appealing to students because it incorporates manipulatives, even at the high-school level, in the assessment process.

STEP BY STEP

- Copy the Signal Cards reproducible on page 147 onto card stock, making enough copies so that each student has a full set. Cut the cards apart, laminate them, and give each student a set that includes one card for "Yes," one for "No," and one for "Maybe."

- Explain to students that when you ask a question, you're not looking for them to raise their hands. Instead, you want each student to hold up the appropriate card so you can see if he knows the answer.

- Pose a question about the material you've been studying. Turn to one of those students holding up a "Yes" card and ask her to give the answer. This indicates to students that you're going to hold them accountable for what they say they know.

NOW LOOK WHAT YOU'VE DONE!

This wasn't so hard, was it? You're still working with the whole class. But in just a few minutes, you've assessed all of your students—not just the ones who were waving their hands in the air. You've figured out who knows what, or at least who *thinks* they know what. And now you have a basis for differentiating your instruction.

Exit Cards

With this formative assessment, students are demonstrating understanding by writing about what they've learned. But that doesn't mean they're just writing a traditional report.

STEP BY STEP

- Give each student an index card.
- Provide students with a prompt or question to be answered as they leave the classroom at the end of the period.
- Use the information on these "exit cards" to inform your instruction the next day. Based on the responses you get on the exit cards, you may decide that you need to have a "coaching clinic" with a small group of students.
- Write down two differences between the circulatory and nervous systems and two similarities between the circulatory and nervous systems.

NOW LOOK WHAT YOU'VE DONE!

This strategy gives students a chance to use their writing skills to indicate their understanding of the material. It also gets them reflecting on what they've learned and helps you evaluate in which content areas they're ready to move on and in which ones they need your help.

FOR EXAMPLE

What might you ask students to respond to on those index cards? Questions can be very broad or a little more specific. Here are some possibilities:

- One thing I learned today was . . .
- If a new student joined the class tomorrow, here is what I would tell the student we are learning:
- Here is how I can use what I learned today.
- Here is how what I'm learning relates to something else I've learned.

> Today I learned how to . . . set a volleyball.

> I am learning how to . . . use light and shadow to create depth in my art.

> I can use what I learned today . . . to be better informed when I vote for the first time next month.

Student Self-Assessment

Use any of these three strategies to help students in self-assessment and in maintaining their own records of their progress.

TAKE YOUR CHOICE

- **How Am I Doing?** Provide each student with a copy of the How Am I Doing reproducible on page 148. Explain that each student is to use that work sheet as a framework for reflecting on and assessing his work at the end of the class period.

- **Rubrics:** Rubrics help students understand what is expected and required in learning, as well as what needs to be done to reach the highest levels of achievement. Rubrics work best if this type of assessment is in the students' hands so they can have ownership of their learning. To be sure students understand what's expected, give them copies of an appropriate writing rubric. Or have the students themselves help generate the quality standards for the assignment and then work in groups to design the rubric.

- **Portfolios:** Portfolios are not just a bunch of student work crammed into a folder. Rather, they offer the basis for feedback that students need in order to be involved in assessment. A portfolio is a collection of student work over time. It contains initial samples of efforts such as writing, plus other pieces that are added later to document progress. Often teachers and students collaborate in deciding what needs to be added. Creating a portfolio like this helps students see the progress they make, and it helps *you* to see how instruction needs to be adjusted to encourage student growth.

NOW LOOK WHAT YOU'VE DONE!

With each of these three strategies, you're making sure students understand what's expected and then giving them a chance to measure their individual progress along the way. Those concepts are at the heart of differentiated instruction.

Reproducible

Chapter Four, Strategy #8

How Am I Doing?

Name of student: _____

Date: _____

The mark on the continuum below represents how well I succeeded in meeting my learning goals today.

Did not do my best

Met my learning goals

Here is what I accomplished: _____

Here is my plan for tomorrow. _____

148

Three Facts & a Fib

This is a summative assessment. You're used to summative assessments. Those are the things you include at the end of the instructional unit so that you can make decisions about student achievement and the success of your instruction. But this summative assessment is a little different because it involves finding ways to honor the differences among your learners. It allows for letting your students show you what they know in many different ways.

We so often rely on the traditional paper-and-pencil fill-in-the-blank, true/false, and multiple-choice questions. But those really reflect only a very narrow range of thinking. In a differentiated classroom, students are active participants, often generating responses that require higher levels of thinking than what's called for in more simple questions. This strategy gives you some options for encouraging more of those student-generated responses.

STEP BY STEP

- Ask each student to write on a piece of paper four statements about any content the class has studied. Three of the statements should be true and one should be false.

- Tell students that each of them should move about the room, sharing her list of statements with others.

- Explain that each student should ask his fellow students to try to pick the false statement on his paper.

- Add that if a student fools another student, the one who was fooled should sign the paper of the student who fooled him.

- When all students have examined each other's papers, have them return to their seats.

- Ask each student to count the number of signatures she collected.

- Compare signature counts to find out who was able to fool the most students.

A FUN INTRODUCTION

To introduce this strategy, try modeling it at the personal level. In other words, make up four statements about yourself—three true and one not. Let each student guess which one is not true of you. Then let each student make up four statements about himself, three true and one not true. Let students see how many people they can fool. This makes a nice get-acquainted activity at the beginning of the school year.

NOW LOOK WHAT YOU'VE DONE!

This strategy gives students important experience in narrowing choices. It also provides a great review and helps you to see who "got" what.

Learning Logs & Response Journals

A learning log is a type of student journal that is generally oriented toward subject matter; it's typically used in the content areas to summarize learning, record observations, explain how a problem was solved, list vocabulary terms, or show diagrams or maps.

A response journal consists entirely of a student's writing; in it, the student records personal responses to literature she's reading. The student might reflect on characters, events, or other literary elements of the literature she's exploring.

Learning logs and response journals are both means of helping students understand and manipulate content. You can use either as part of a summative assessment. You can also differentiate them.

SUPPORT YOUR STRUGGLING WRITERS

You can also differentiate learning logs and response journals in a way that supports those students who struggle with writing their responses. All you need to do is invest in a bound composition journal and ask a local office-supply store to cut it in half horizontally. This will create little learning logs or response journals, making them less overwhelming for your students.

STEP BY STEP

- Learning logs and response journals typically involve responses to prompts—but there's no reason every student has to be responding to the same prompt. If the class is studying heroes, you could give some students blue index cards with a prompt that asks, "What purposes do heroes serve?"

- You might give other students yellow index cards with the prompt, "Rank your three greatest heroes in literature and explain your ranking."

- In this way you're differentiating the learning log/response journal assignments according to students' readiness.

NOW LOOK WHAT YOU'VE DONE!

This is a great example of differentiation within a whole-group setting. All students are involved in the same activity at the same time, but their specific instructions vary according to their levels of readiness.

Four Square Products

Four Square Products honor the varied learning styles in your classroom while allowing all your students to demonstrate what they've learned.

STEP BY STEP

- Create a menu of ways students can show you what they've learned without relying on paper/pencil responses. Use the Four Square Products reproducible on page 149 as a guide. Three of the four squares represent ways students learn: visually, auditorily, and kinesthetically. The fourth square gives options for written products.

- Develop a rubric to assess very different products according to the same quality standards. Categories might include effort, thoroughness, originality, and the quality of the finished product.

- Let students choose from the listed options to show you what they've learned.

NOW LOOK WHAT YOU'VE DONE!

It's important to think beyond state and national tests to ongoing classroom measures. These can include traditional formal assessments, observations, and homework, as well as more authentic types of assessments, such as portfolios, rubrics, student self-evaluations, demonstrations, conferences, learning logs,

response journals, and projects. Giving students choices is a key piece of differentiated instruction because it plays to the strengths of individual students, allowing each student to demonstrate understanding of the content in his own way.

Reproducible

Chapter Four, Strategy #11

Four Square Products

VISUAL	AUDITORY
Advertisement	Audiotape
Collage	News broadcast
Poster	Speech
Flowchart	Debate
Venn diagram	Lecture
Painting	Group discussion
Map	Interview
Video	Round table discussion
Story map	Book review
Timeline	Teach others
T chart	

KINESTHETIC	WRITTEN
A model	Book report
Performance of a dance	Letter
or skit	Poetry
Sculpture	Research paper
Mobile	Story
Diorama	Checklist
Dramatization	Journal
Experiment	Essay
Pantomime	Newsletter
Role play	Survey
Display	

149

Kinesthetic Assessment

This strategy asks students to create sentences that reflect content studied. Students like the element of chance that's involved.

STEP BY STEP

• Start with a set of nine index cards for each student. On each card, write a vocabulary term from the content the class is studying. (Or fill in a copy of the Kinesthetic Assessment reproducible on page 150, run off copies on card stock, and cut the cards apart.)

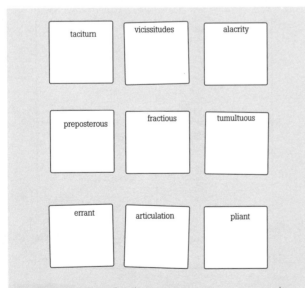

tacitum	vicissitudes	alacrity
preposterous	fractious	tumultuous
errant	articulation	pliant

Some mistook Gina's taciturn nature to mean she was extremely pliant, when in fact she was just as fractious as the rest of us.

I knew it was preposterous to think the crowd was fractious because I had seen what a tumultuous welcome they had given their hero.

• Give a complete set to each student.

• Each student shuffles his cards and lays them out in a grid pattern, with three rows of three cards each.

• Each student writes eight sentences using the words. Three sentences must use the words in the three horizontal rows (one sentence for the words in each row); three sentences must use the words in the vertical columns (again, one sentence for each); and two sentences must use the three-card diagonals (one left to right and one right to left).

NOW LOOK WHAT YOU'VE DONE

When you use this strategy, students are creating the sentences and not responding to a true/false or multiple-choice teacher-created assessment. Manipulating the cards allows for kinesthetic involvement. You can use the same words for all students, or you can further differentiate by selecting different words for certain individuals or groups.

Synectics

Synectics asks students to compare things not usually compared. It provides the opportunity for students to process information at higher levels and it invites creativity.

STEP BY STEP

- Break students into groups of three or four.
- Each group appoints a recorder.
- Each group chooses a random category such as sports, movies, or household objects.
- The group brainstorms a list of four items that fit their category. For the category of household objects, items might include an oven, a television, a chair, and a lightbulb.
- The recorder for the group lists the items on a piece of paper.
- Write on the board the following sentence: "_____ is like a _____ because _____."
- Fill in the subject of the sentence based on content the class is studying. Maybe you say, "Photosynthesis is like _____ because _____."
- Ask each group to brainstorm ways to complete the sentence. For example, students might say, "Photosynthesis is like an oven (object from the category of household objects) because it makes something new."
- Allow three to five minutes for brainstorming.
- Ask each group to pick its favorite analogy to share aloud with the rest of the class.

NOW LOOK WHAT YOU'VE DONE

You're giving students the opportunity to enhance their understanding of content in a meaningful way because they're summarizing information as they create the analogies. This is much more effective than just reading a chapter in a textbook and answering the questions at the end.

A MANAGEMENT TIP

Work with students to establish rules, responsibilities, and procedures for the classroom. Then practice those things with the students. If a rule for the classroom is "Students come to class ready to learn," discuss with students what that might look like. Maybe the class will decide that students need to come with homework and necessary supplies each day, arrive on time, etc.

The Tournament

The Tournament is an integrating and organizing assessment strategy that asks students to name, compare, sort, and synthesize key learning. Students use a graphic organizer similar to one used to determine a champion through elimination rounds of a sports tournament.

STEP BY STEP

- Break students into groups of three or four.
- Give each of the groups a copy of the Tournament graphic organizer on page 151.
- Each group appoints a recorder.

- The group brainstorms eight words about any topic they've been studying.
- The recorder writes one of the words next to each number on the graphic organizer.
- Students then choose one word from each "bracket" to be the winner or more important of the two.
- They continue narrowing down their choices from each pair until they reach the one they agree is the most important word.
- Each group shares and defends its choice for the most important word.

NOW LOOK WHAT YOU'VE DONE

Students have the opportunity to go from small-group to full-class interaction as they process the content studied.

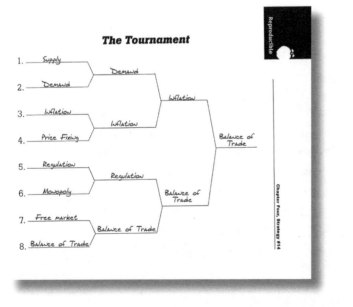

The Tournament

Now It's Your Turn to Reflect on This Chapter

What is your "aha!" or insight or thinking after reading this chapter?

_____

_____

_____

_____

_____

What strategy will you try first? How will you use it in your classroom?

_____

_____

_____

_____

How and why might you tailor one of the strategies in this chapter to meet the needs of a specific student or students?

_____

_____

5

Getting Started

Wow! You've finished reading and reflecting on ideas for beginning (or continuing) your journey into differentiation. Just maybe I've given you the courage to take those next steps. Differentiation really is an extension of good teaching, but it does have some complexity to it.

You know how I've been saying that your students will eventually give up if they don't experience some success? Well, you're likely to give up on differentiation if you don't start to experience some success with it where you are comfortable—in your whole-group setting. I hope you can see some clear windows of opportunity to work differentiation into your classroom and to help your individual students, even while you're still teaching in a whole-group setting.

Change is hard—any kind of change, whether you perceive it to be a good change or a bad change. I remember a time when I

was leaving one school to open another, new school. I had served as principal at the old school for a number of years. I perceived the opportunity to open the new school as a positive change, but it was still change, and it was difficult to let go of something I was comfortable with in order to try something new. Knowing this, the president of the Parent Teacher Organization made a wall hanging for me. On that wall hanging was a quote that I refer to over and over again when faced with change: "It is possible to change without improving, but it is impossible to improve without changing."

Hold that thought as you begin the journey into honoring all the diversity in your classroom.

LET'S GET GOING!

As you continue to differentiate in your classroom, be sure to:

- Acknowledge what you're already doing.
- Begin with simple strategies that are easy to implement.
- Build a circle of support with other teachers.
- Celebrate your successes.
- Learn from your mistakes.
- Keep the students first.

Reproducibles

Reproducible

Appointment Calendar

NAME: _____

8:00 a.m._____   3:30 p.m._____

8:30 a.m._____   4:00 p.m._____

9:00 a.m._____   4:30 p.m._____

9:30 a.m._____   5:00 p.m._____

10:00 a.m._____   5:30 p.m._____

10:30 a.m._____   6:00 p.m._____

11:00 a.m._____   6:30 p.m._____

11:30 a.m._____   7:00 p.m._____

12:00 noon _____   7:30 p.m._____

12:30 p.m._____   8:00 p.m._____

1:00 p.m._____   8:30 p.m._____

1:30 p.m._____   9:00 p.m._____

2:00 p.m._____   9:30 p.m._____

2:30 p.m._____   10:00 p.m._____

3:00 p.m._____   10:30 p.m._____

eproducible

The Parking Lot

Name: _____

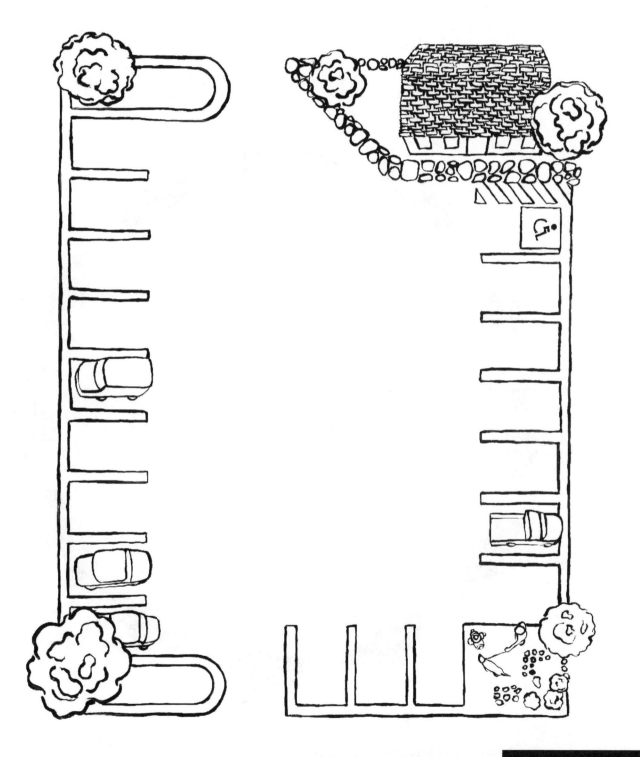

Reproducible

Geometric Questions

Name: _____

Questions That Keep Going Around in My Head

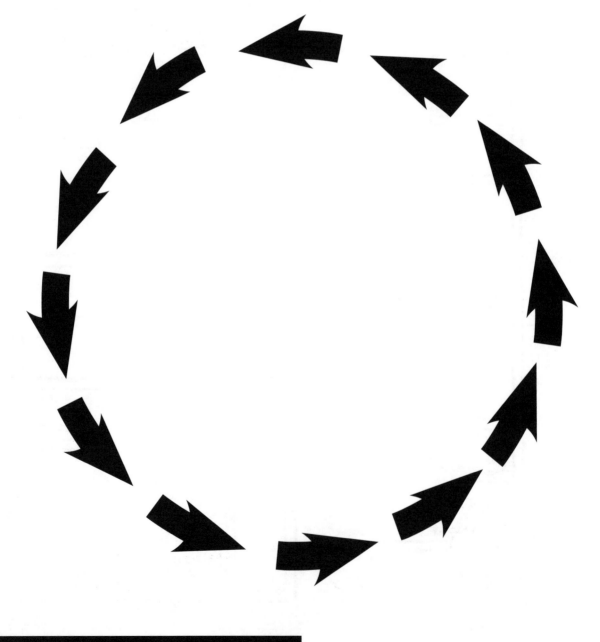

eproducible

Key Words & Sample Questions
from Bloom's Taxonomy

LEVEL 1: KNOWLEDGE

Recalling basic facts, concepts, and terms

Key Words: Define, describe, label, list, match, memorize, recall, recite, record, select, show, tell, what, when, where, who, why, write

Sample Questions:

- Which one . . . ?
- List . . .
- Name the . . .
- When did _____ happen?
- How much . . . ?

Example: List 20 major events from the Cold War.

LEVEL 2: COMPREHENSION

Demonstrating or showing understanding of facts and ideas

Key Words: Classify, compare, contrast, demonstrate, explain, express, infer, locate, outline, paraphrase, restate, review, rewrite, show, summarize

Sample Questions:

- What is the main idea of . . . ?
- Which statements support . . . ?
- Give an example of . . .
- Explain the reasons . . .

Example: Explain the reasons for the Cuban Missile Crisis.

LEVEL 3: APPLICATION

Applying knowledge to new or unfamiliar situations; using what has been learned

Key Words: Apply, associate, build, calculate, construct, develop, diagram, display, dramatize, draw, illustrate, integrate, interpret, interview, make, model, paint, plan, reformat, research, solve

Sample Questions:

- How would you use . . . ?
- What examples can you find to . . . ?
- Tell what would happen if . . .
- Predict what might happen if . . .

Example: Predict what might have happened afterward if the Bay of Pigs invasion had been successful.

Reproducible

LEVEL 4: ANALYSIS

Examining and breaking information into parts

Key Words: Analyze, categorize, classify, compare, contrast, debate, diagram, discover, distinguish, illustrate, inspect, investigate, question, separate, simplify, solve, study, take apart

Sample Questions:

• How would you classify . . . ?

• How would you categorize . . . ?

• Can you critique . . . ?

• Make a distinction . . .

• Separate the facts and the opinions.

Example: Investigate the way that the Cold War was manifested in numerous "hot" proxy wars.

LEVEL 5: SYNTHESIS

Putting information together in new ways; combining content into a pattern that is different

Key Words: Adapt, build, compose, construct, create, design, discuss, form, imagine, invent, make, prepare, produce, transform

Sample Questions:

• Propose an alternative . . .

• How else would you . . .

• What way would you design . . . ?

• Write a new ending . . .

Example: Construct economic models for post–Soviet republics that are sustainable and account for the legacy of the Cold War and the rise of China as an economic power.

LEVEL 6: EVALUATION

Making judgments about information; evaluating based on a set of criteria

Key Words: Argue, assess, conclude, debate, defend, dispute, estimate, forecast, formulate, interpret, judge, prove, recommend

Sample Questions:

• What is your opinion of . . . ?

• What choice would you have made . . . ?

• Based on your knowledge, how would you explain . . . ?

• Find the errors . . .

• Rate the . . .

Example: Assess the social, economic, security, and political climate resulting from the Cold War.

Reproducible

For Visual Learners

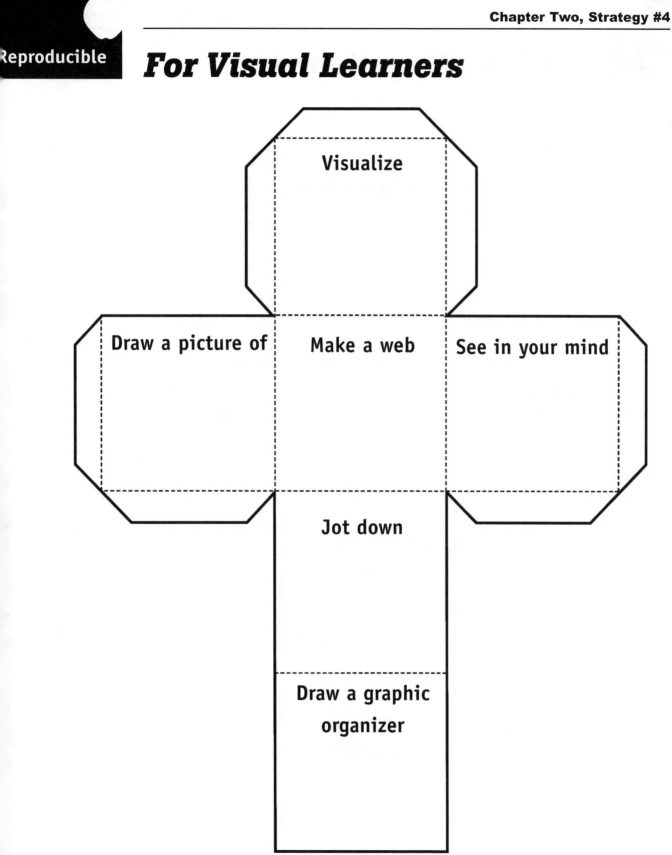

Visualize

Draw a picture of | Make a web | See in your mind

Jot down

Draw a graphic organizer

Reproducible

For Auditory Learners

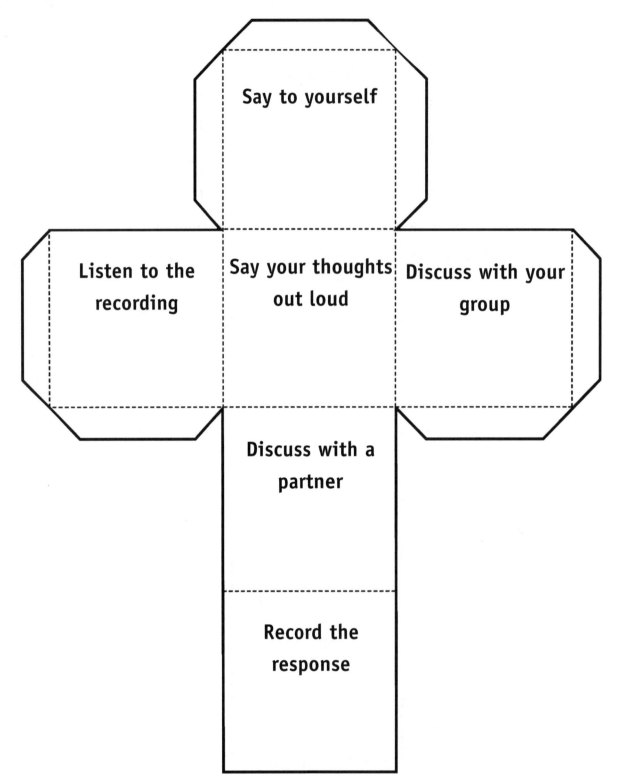

Say to yourself

Listen to the recording

Say your thoughts out loud

Discuss with your group

Discuss with a partner

Record the response

Reproducible

For Kinesthetic Learners

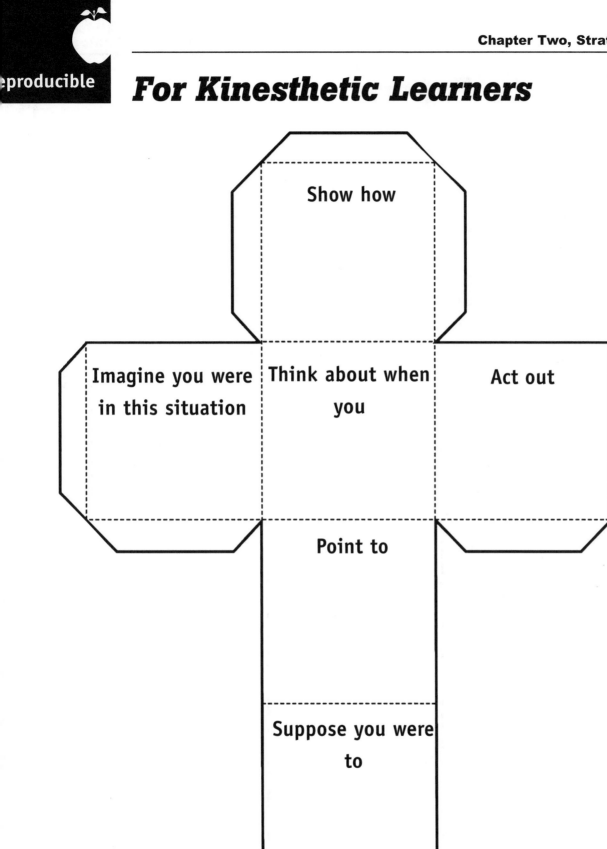

Show how

Imagine you were in this situation

Think about when you

Act out

Point to

Suppose you were to

Reproducible

Cube Pattern

eproducible

Bloom's Cube

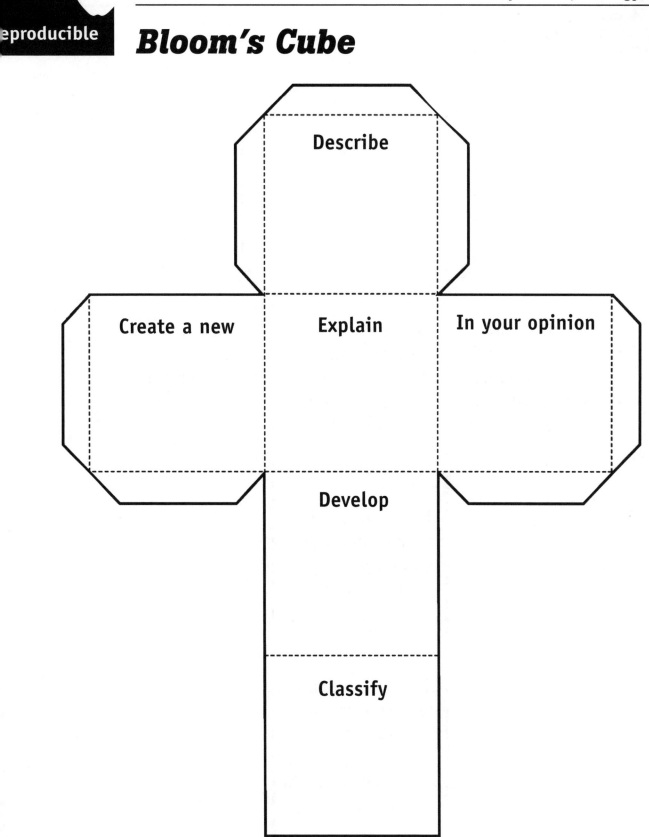

Reproducible

Math Cube

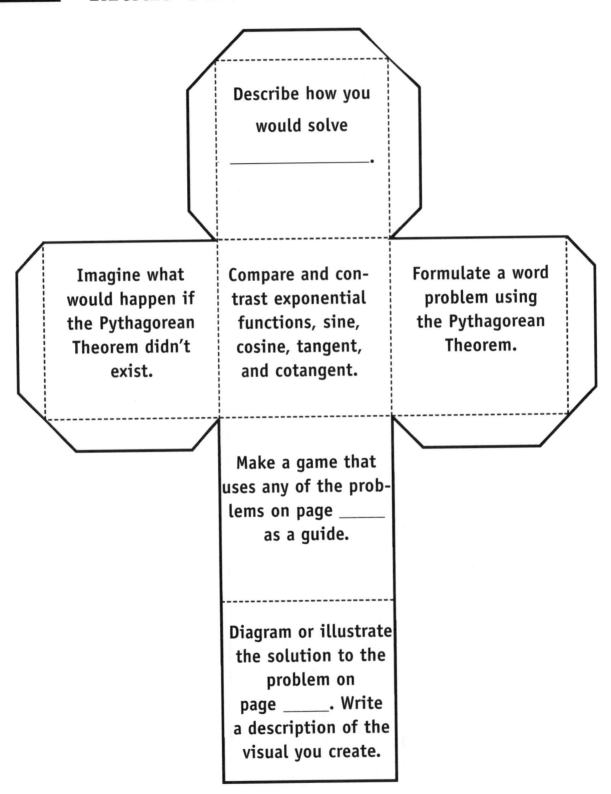

Describe how you would solve

_____.

Imagine what would happen if the Pythagorean Theorem didn't exist.

Compare and contrast exponential functions, sine, cosine, tangent, and cotangent.

Formulate a word problem using the Pythagorean Theorem.

Make a game that uses any of the problems on page _____ as a guide.

Diagram or illustrate the solution to the problem on page _____. Write a description of the visual you create.

eproducible

Comprehension Cube

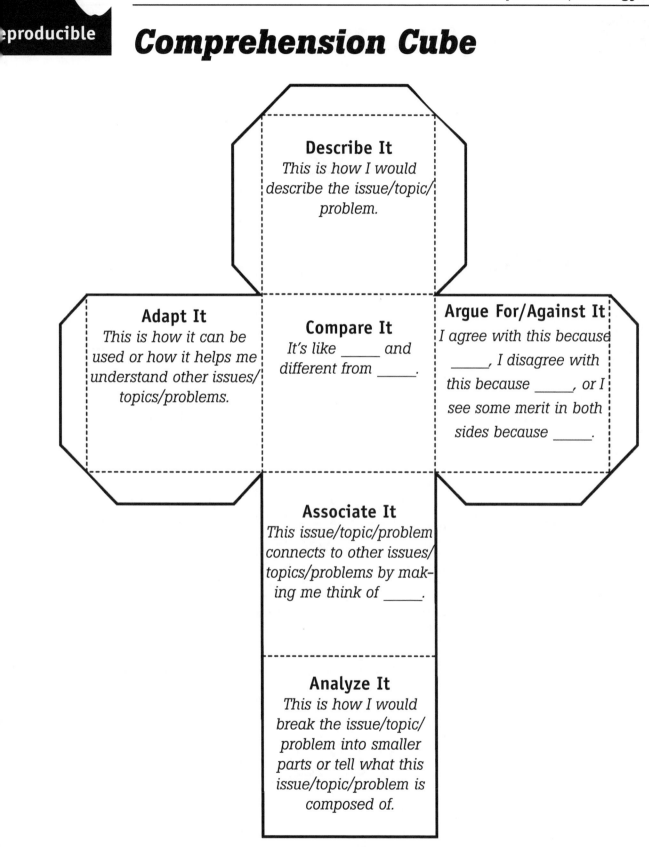

Describe It
This is how I would describe the issue/topic/ problem.

Adapt It
This is how it can be used or how it helps me understand other issues/ topics/problems.

Compare It
It's like _____ and different from _____.

Argue For/Against It
I agree with this because _____, I disagree with this because _____, or I see some merit in both sides because _____.

Associate It
This issue/topic/problem connects to other issues/ topics/problems by making me think of _____.

Analyze It
This is how I would break the issue/topic/ problem into smaller parts or tell what this issue/topic/problem is composed of.

Reproducible

I Have/Who Has?

I Have Who Has	I Have Who Has	I Have Who Has
I Have Who Has	I Have Who Has	I Have Who Has
I Have Who Has	I Have Who Has	I Have Who Has

reproducible

Question-Tac-Toe

Knowledge *(Write, List, Define, Label)*	**Comprehension** *(Explain, Compare, Summarize)*	**Application** *(Apply, Illustrate, Diagram)*
Analysis *(Analyze, Categorize, Solve)*	**Synthesis** *(Adapt, Compose, Create)*	**Evaluation** *(Judge, Recommend, Forecast)*
Comprehension *(Outline)*	**Evaluation** *(Debate)*	**Synthesis** *(Compose)*

Reproducible

Question-Tac-Toe
For Visual Learners

Knowledge *(Record)*	**Comprehension** *(Locate)*	**Application** *(Calculate)*
Analysis *(Simplify)*	**Synthesis** *(Imagine)*	**Evaluation** *(Prove)*
Synthesis *(Prepare)*	**Evaluation** *(Assess)*	**Comprehension** *(Rewrite)*

Reproducible

Question-Tac-Toe
For Auditory Learners

Knowledge *(Recall)*	**Comprehension** *(Explain)*	**Application** *(Interpret)*
Analysis *(Debate)*	**Synthesis** *(Create and Discuss)*	**Evaluation** *(Defend)*
Analysis *(Question)*	**Application** *(Interview)*	**Comprehension** *(Express)*

Reproducible

Question-Tac-Toe
For Kinesthetic Learners

Knowledge *(Label)*	**Comprehension** *(Show)*	**Application** *(Draw)*
Analysis *(Diagram)*	**Synthesis** *(Construct)*	**Evaluation** *(Argue by Acting Out)*
Synthesis *(Make)*	**Application** *(Paint)*	**Analysis** *(Categorize)*

eproducible

Question-Answer Relationships

LEVEL I
In-the-Book Questions

Right There

LEVEL II
In-the-Book Questions

Think, Search, and Find

LEVEL III
In-My-Head Questions

Author and Me

LEVEL IV
In-My-Head Questions

On My Own

Reproducible

Q.A.R. Level I Questions

RIGHT THERE
(TEXTUALLY EXPLICIT)

ATTRIBUTES OF LEVEL I QUESTIONS

1. The answer is usually contained in one sentence and is easy to find.

2. Often the same words that make up the answer are found in the question.

3. The reader needs only literal thinking to answer the question.

Adapted from the work of Taffy E. Raphael 2006

eproducible

Q.A.R. Level II Questions

THINK, SEARCH, AND FIND
(TEXTUALLY IMPLICIT)

PUTTING THE PARTS TOGETHER
ATTRIBUTES OF LEVEL II QUESTIONS

1. The answer is found in more than one place. The parts must be put together to answer the question.

2. Certain words—including pointer/signal words, plurals, and conjunctions—indicate that the answer is in more than one place.

3. The words in the question may or may not be the same words used to answer the question.

4. The reader needs only literal thinking to answer the question.

Adapted from the work of Taffy E. Raphael 2006

Reproducible

Q.A.R. Level III Questions

AUTHOR AND ME
(SCRIPT IMPLICIT)

ATTRIBUTES OF LEVEL III QUESTIONS

1. The reader must read the text to answer the question (text dependent).

2. The reader must use inferential thinking in order to answer the question.

3. The reader relies on prior knowledge and experience.

4. The reader must look for clues and evidence (prove the answer with details).

5. The reader must read between the lines as the answer is not explicit in the text.

Adapted from the work of Taffy E. Raphael 2006

eproducible

Q.A.R. Level IV Questions

ON MY OWN

BEYOND THE TEXT

ATTRIBUTES OF LEVEL IV QUESTIONS

1. The reader need not read the text in order to answer the question.

2. The reader must use inferential thinking.

3. The reader relies on prior knowledge and experiences.

4. The reader must use his own ideas and opinions to answer the questions.

Adapted from the work of Taffy E. Raphael 2006

Reproducible

118 T.H.I.N.K. Questions

T (THOUGHTS/FEELINGS/OPINION/POINT OF VIEW)

• How do you feel when no one laughs at your jokes?

• Which day of the week are you the happiest?

• What time of day is your favorite?

• What is your opinion of homework?

• What is your parents' opinion of homework?

• Be the head secretary for the U.N. for one day. Tell what you do.

• If the ozone layer could talk, what would it say?

• What would your journal say if it could talk?

• Pretend you are the principal. Describe your best day.

• What would you change if you were the teacher for one day?

• Be a pencil. Tell why you are better than a pen.

• You are (character from a book). What is your best (worst) memory?

• Pretend you are a grizzly bear. Who is your best friend?

• You are a trick question in math. What is the question?

• Two cars in the student parking lot are having a conversation. What are they saying?

• What would protons say to neutrons?

• Do you ever feel sad when you laugh?

• Do you ever feel happy when you cry?

H (HOW COME?)

• How come the president of the United States is not elected by popular vote?

• How come people in different regions of the United States speak English with different accents?

• How come a toaster has a setting that burns the toast?

• How come pushing the elevator button over and over again doesn't make it go faster?

• How come companies outsource labor to other countries? Isn't shipping expensive?

• How come students don't have lunch duty?

• How come teachers send home papers with red marks and not yellow marks?

• How come you get in trouble for "talking back" to the teacher? Aren't you supposed to do that?

• How come a teacher can tell if a holiday is coming without looking at a calendar?

• How come people don't drive more fuel-efficient cars if those kinds of cars are available?

• How come you fill in a form by filling it out?

• How come there's not an egg in eggplant?

• How come U.S. high school tracks are different from college tracks and from tracks in the rest of the world?

• How come you set your alarm to go off when you really want it to go on?

• How come water boils quickly unless you watch it?

• How come experience is the best teacher?

• How come a dog is a man's best friend?

• How come the Olympics change location each time?

• How come we aren't extracting very much oil from the oil shale in Colorado?

• How come a whole bag of light and fluffy marshmallows makes you gain weight?

I (WHAT IF?)

• What if you only went to school on Saturdays?

• What if you lived where the story took place?

• What if computers didn't exist?

• What if all food tasted the same?

• What if there were no classroom rules?

• What if there were no chocolate?

• What if water didn't freeze?

• What if you awoke and you were 7 feet tall?

• What if there were no desks at school?

• What if water had an expiration date?

• What if you had eyes in the back of your head?

• What if you could travel at the speed of light?

• What if you could feel the earth rotating?

• What if you were invisible?

• What if women weren't paid less (on average) for doing the same jobs as men?

• What if the war on terrorism never ends?

• What if Quebec achieves national sovereignty?

• What if the Endangered Species Act had not been passed?

• What if the United States were more multilingual?

• What if local government received more prominence in the media?

• What if people reduced their television watching by 50 percent?

• What if a majority of school districts adopted mandatory school uniforms?

• What if the earth were not tilted on its axis?

• What if we could develop a carbon-dioxide-neutral energy power plant?

• What if we could predict earthquakes, volcanic eruptions, and tsunamis?

• What if we genetically modify the vegetables we eat?

N (NAME AND NEXT)

• Name all the ways you could say "Great!"

• A hurricane has destroyed the trees in your yard. What do you do next?

• Name all the ways you could communicate if you couldn't talk.

• The saying goes, "When in Rome, do as the Romans do." Name all the things you wouldn't do in Rome.

• 1, 2, 3, 5, 8, 13 . . . What comes next?

• Name all the uses for a paper clip.

• Name all the good things about homework.

• You wake up during the night and smell smoke. What do you do next?

• Name all the ways you can think of to convince your friend to drink a glass of buttermilk.

• Name all the ways to use a toothpick.

• Name all the words you can make from the word "unbelievable."

• Name all the reasons you can why it might be good to be early to something.

• Name all the questions you can add to this list of T.H.I.N.K. questions.

• Name all the reasons for more gun control.

• Name all the reasons for less gun control.

• Name all the reasons for economic growth.

• Name all the reasons for regulation of economic growth.

• An oil tanker spills crude oil in Prince William Sound, Alaska. What do you do next?

• A presidential administration is accused of corruption or illegal acts. What do you do next?

• A viral disease becomes pandemic. What do you do next?

• You discover a cure for H.I.V. What do you do next?

• Name all the reasons for keeping the Electoral College.

• Name all the reasons for abolishing the Electoral College.

• You are not accepted to college. What do you do next?

• Your job is outsourced. What do you do next?

- Name all the reasons for restricting the international trade in human organs.
- Name all the reasons for allowing the international trade in human organs.
- Name all the reasons for getting involved in international territorial disputes.
- Name all the reasons for staying out of international territorial disputes.
- Name all the reasons for signing the Kyoto Protocol.
- Name all the reasons for not signing the Kyoto Protocol.
- Name all the reasons for developing nuclear energy.
- Name all the reasons for not developing nuclear energy.
- Name all the reasons for pursuing stem cell research.
- Name all the reasons for restricting stem cell research.
- Name the advantages of wind-generated electricity.
- SARS strikes again. What do you do next?

K (KIND OF ALIKE AND KIND OF DIFFERENT)

- How are you different from your siblings?
- How is running the same as a ruler?
- How are you different from your parents?
- How are a race car and the president alike?
- How are risk and change alike?
- How is planning your weekend like solving a problem?
- How is gossiping about your friends like writing a story?
- How are an explorer and an artist different?
- How are school and a bagel alike?
- How is school different from a party?
- How are the geography of Mexico and the geography of Saudi Arabia alike?
- How are the Japanese Archipelago, the Mediterranean, the Caribbean Isles, and the Malay Archipelago alike?
- How is the American Dream examined in *The Great Gatsby* different from the American Dream examined in *A Raisin in the Sun?*
- How are the Cascade Range in Washington and the Southern Alps in New Zealand alike?
- How is Santiago Calatrava's Turning Torso apartment building like a human spine?
- How are the major world religions alike? How are they different?
- How is the book version of _____ like the movie version? How is it different?

Reproducible

Talk with F.R.E.D.

Facts, Reflections, Evaluation, Decisions

FACTS

- What scenes or images do you remember?
- What bits of conversation do you remember?
- What facts do you remember?
- What other things did you observe?
- What facts do you know about _____?

REFLECTIONS

- What was your first response to the scenes, etc.?
- Were you excited? Curious? Nervous?
- How did you feel when you watched the video or read the text?

EVALUATION

- What were the most significant events?
- Was this book or video important to you? Why or why not?
- What was your greatest insight, or what was the biggest thing you learned?
- What was the most interesting part for you? Why?

DECISIONS

- What would you say about this text or video to someone who's not here?
- What decisions would you make now that you've read this text or watched this video?
- Would you recommend this to another student? Why or why not?

eproducible

Five Questions to Ask

NAME:_____

1. VISUALIZATION: What mental pictures do I see?

_____

_____

2. CONNECTIONS: What does this remind me of?

_____

_____

3. INFERENCE: What do I know now, even though I wasn't told the information in the text?

_____

_____

4. PREDICTION: What might happen next?

_____

_____

5. SUMMARIZATION/CONCLUSIONS: What was this mostly about?

_____

_____

Reproducible

How Well Did We Work Together?

Group Name: _____

Discuss each statement with your group members, reach agreement, and make a check on the appropriate line.

	NOT MUCH	A LOT
We listened to each other.	_____	_____
We shared the work.	_____	_____
We all participated by giving our ideas.	_____	_____
We encouraged each other by asking questions.	_____	_____
We brought out the best in each other.	_____	_____

BRIEFLY ANSWER EACH OF THE FOLLOWING:

We learned this about ourselves or about working

together. _____

_____

Another time, this is one thing we would do differently.

_____

_____

eproducible

Group Norms

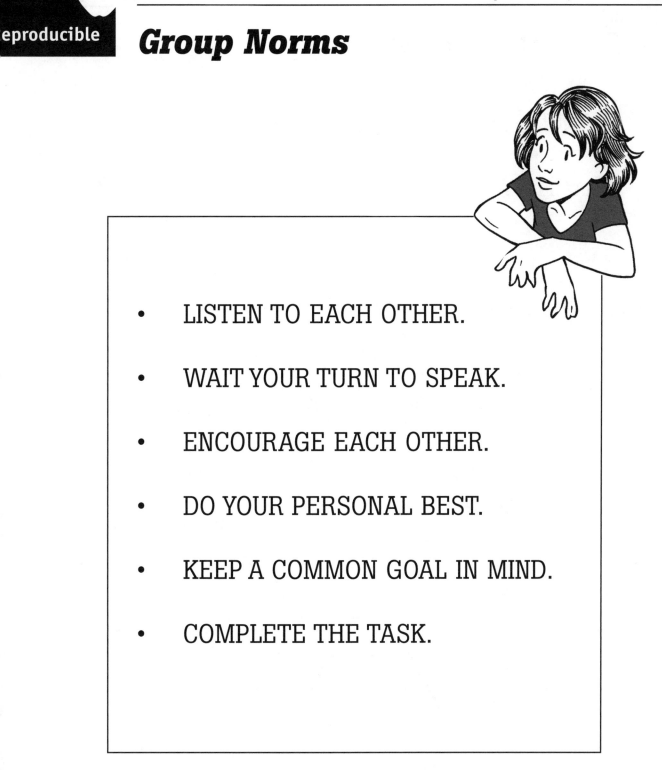

- LISTEN TO EACH OTHER.

- WAIT YOUR TURN TO SPEAK.

- ENCOURAGE EACH OTHER.

- DO YOUR PERSONAL BEST.

- KEEP A COMMON GOAL IN MIND.

- COMPLETE THE TASK.

Reproducible

Concept Map

NAME: _____

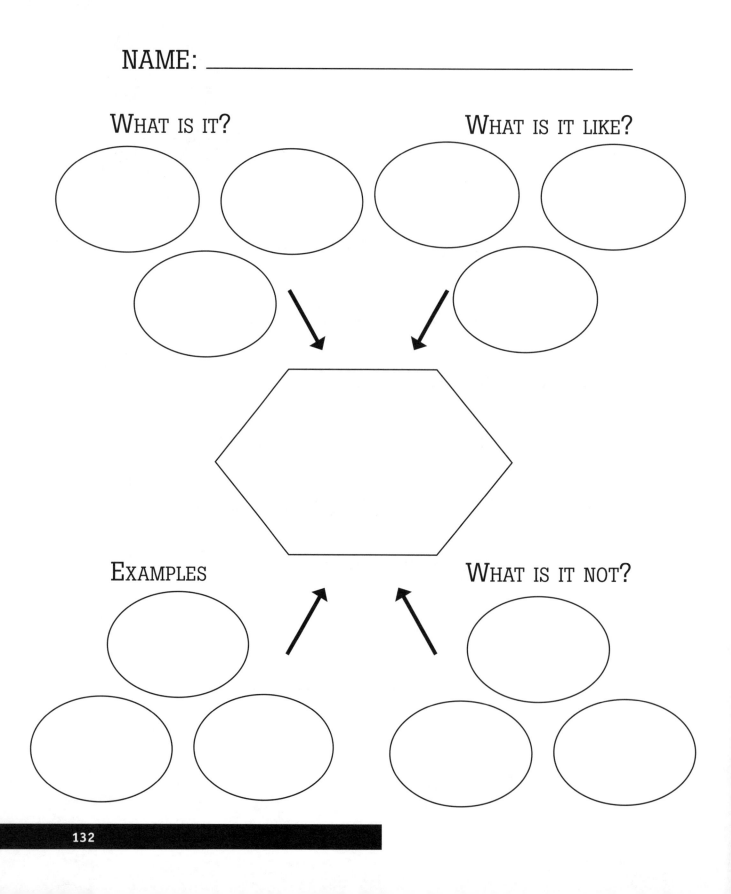

WHAT IS IT?

WHAT IS IT LIKE?

EXAMPLES

WHAT IS IT NOT?

Reproducible

Brainstorming A–Z

NAME: _____

SUBJECT: _____

A _____	N _____
B _____	O _____
C _____	P _____
D _____	Q _____
E _____	R _____
F _____	S _____
G _____	T _____
H _____	U _____
I _____	V _____
J _____	W _____
K _____	X _____
L _____	Y _____
M _____	Z _____

Reproducible

Role Cards for a Lecture or Video

QUESTION ASKER

Responsible for asking a question of the others in the group about the content of the video or lecture

SUMMARIZER

Responsible for telling the other students the main points of the video or lecture

I AGREE WITH . . .

Responsible for discussing those points you agreed with in the video or lecture

I DISAGREE WITH OR I WAS SURPRISED BY . . .

Responsible for discussing those points you disagreed with or were surprised to learn in the video or lecture

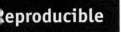
Reproducible

Pointer/Signal Words

SEQUENCE TEXT STRUCTURE:
first, next, then, finally

DESCRIPTIVE TEXT STRUCTURE:
for example, to illustrate, such as, for instance

PROBLEM AND SOLUTION TEXT STRUCTURE:
dilemma, problem, puzzle, solved, the question is

COMPARE AND CONTRAST TEXT STRUCTURE:
alike, different from, same as, versus, similar to

CAUSE AND EFFECT TEXT STRUCTURE:
if . . . then, as a result, therefore, because

Reproducible

Blue Role Cards
for Expository Text

MAIN IDEA MINDER
Responsible for telling the main idea of the text

DETAIL PERSON
Responsible for giving several details from the text

KEY WORD FINDER
Responsible for identifying key words in the text and being ready to explain to the group what they mean

QUESTION ASKER
Responsible for generating a question about the text that can be answered directly by reading the text

MAIN IDEA MINDER
Responsible for telling the main idea of the text

DETAIL PERSON
Responsible for giving several details from the text

KEY WORD FINDER
Responsible for identifying key words in the text and being ready to explain to the group what they mean

QUESTION ASKER
Responsible for generating a question about the text that can be answered directly by reading the text

eproducible

Green Role Cards
for Expository Text

SIGNAL PERSON
Responsible for identifying signal words and the text structure in which the text is written

DESIGNER
Responsible for drawing a graphic organizer to match the text structure

GRAPHICS GURU
Responsible for discussing how diagrams, charts, etc. help the reader to understand the text

QUESTION ASKER
Responsible for generating a question about the text that cannot be answered directly from reading the text

SIGNAL PERSON
Responsible for identifying signal words and the text structure in which the text is written

DESIGNER
Responsible for drawing a graphic organizer to match the text structure

GRAPHICS GURU
Responsible for discussing how diagrams, charts, etc. help the reader to understand the text

QUESTION ASKER
Responsible for generating a question about the text that cannot be answered directly from reading the text

Reproducible

Discussion Cards
for Narrative Text

CHARACTERS	SETTING
THEME	RESOLUTION
CHARACTERS	SETTING
THEME	RESOLUTION

eproducible

Think-Tac-Toe

Reproducible

Anything-but-Horizontal
Reading-Tac-Toe

FOR SHORT FICTION

Directions: Choose three options that do not form a horizontal Reading-Tac-Toe. Circle your choices.

BEFORE READING	Study the picture on the cover of the book. Make five predictions about how it relates to the short story you've chosen.	Choose a short story to read. Look through the story and pick out two words you don't know at all, two words you think you know, and two words you know. Share all of these with a partner.	Choose a short story to read. Find a partner and share the reasons you selected your story. Explain what you anticipate it will be about and what you already know about the topic.
DURING READING	Use sticky notes to flag at least 20 vocabulary words from this story that are new to you.	In your reading journal, write down key events and what you see emerging explicitly or implicitly about a character with each event.	In your reading journal, note the setting's specific impact on the story and its themes. Use words or pictures.
AFTER READING	Create an artistic rendering that represents the story. Be prepared to explain it to the class.	Conduct a mock interview with another student who read the same story. One of you should take on the role of a character from the story.	Write a review of the story that would be appropriate for publication in a newspaper or magazine.

eproducible

Anything-but-Horizontal Reading-Tac-Toe

FOR EXPOSITORY TEXT

Directions: Choose three options that do not form a horizontal Reading-Tac-Toe. Circle your choices.

BEFORE READING	Look through the text. Find signal words that might indicate the structure of the text. List the words and decide in what structure the text is written.	Look through the text. List the access features (headings, subheadings, charts, graphs, etc.) that you see. Try to determine why specific access features were or were not included.	Pick two subheadings. Change them into questions.
DURING READING	Create a graphic organizer that matches the text structure. Use your graphic organizer to take notes while reading the text.	List some of the questions this text raises. List some questions it answers. Explain in writing how someone might disagree with the point this text makes.	Make a list of words that are unfamiliar to you. Find the definition of each one and write it in your own words. Draw a visual of the word.
AFTER READING	Write a one-page report telling how narrative and expository texts are different from each other.	Write four facts about the text you just read. Make three of the statements true and one not true. See if you can fool other classmates by asking them which one is not true of the text.	Draw a graphic representation of what was important in the text. Use color, pictures, and symbols.

Reproducible

Think-Tac-Toe the MI Way
RESPONDING TO TEXT

Directions: Choose one activity from each line to make a Think-Tac-Toe. Circle your choices.

Write about the main character of your story. Be prepared to present a 10-minute report to the class.	In your journal, create a graphic organizer and use it to compare yourself to the main character.	Think of someone you know who is like one of the characters in the book. Write about how the real-life person and the character in the story are alike.
Draw a picture of the setting of the story.	Make up a rap or song about the setting of the story and set it to music.	Build a model of the setting of the story.
Make a timeline to show the major events in the story. Include visuals.	With a group of three other students, create a new ending for the story.	With a group of three other students, create a skit and act out the story.

eproducible

4-6-8

CHARACTERS	SETTINGS	EVENTS
1. _____	1. _____	1. _____
2. _____	2. _____	2. _____
3. _____	3. _____	3. _____
4. _____	4. _____	4. _____
	5. _____	5. _____
	6. _____	6. _____
		7. _____
		8. _____

Reproducible

Interests, Intelligences & Ignorances Survey

Name: _____ *Date:* _____

• What is your favorite subject in school? Why?

_____

• What is your least favorite subject? Why?

_____

• What do you like to do in your free time?

_____

• What are some of your favorite books? Why?

_____

• What kinds of music do you like? Why?

_____

• What are some of your favorite movies? Why?

_____

• What past school project was your favorite? Why?

_____

Rank the following topics according to what you are interested in:

3 = very interested   2 = somewhat interested   1 = not interested

___ Computers	___ Art	___ Science	___ Dance
___ Sports	___ Drama	___ Social studies	
___ Music	___ Math	___ Writing	___ Reading

How do you think you learn best? (Examples might be when it is quiet, with a friend, etc.)

_____

• If you could learn anything this school year, what would you choose to learn about? Why?

_____

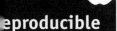
eproducible

Informal Rating Scale to Discover Intelligences

For each of the following statements, check the characteristics that best describe the student. Note the areas in which each student scores the highest number of checks.

Name of student: _____

VERBAL/LINGUISTIC

___ Is highly verbal
___ Has a good memory
___ Writes better than average for age
___ Likes to read and do research
___ Uses accurate spelling
___ Has a good vocabulary for age
___ Enjoys word games
___ Enjoys listening and speaking

VISUAL/SPATIAL

___ Likes art class
___ Is good at drawing
___ Can visualize things
___ Can read a map well
___ Likes working with models
___ Is good at matching colors
___ Thinks in pictures
___ Can find way in the unfamiliar

MUSICAL

___ Likes music class
___ Hums occasionally during class
___ Likes to listen to music
___ Has a good sense of rhythm
___ Can tap out a beat
___ Makes up tunes
___ Is interested in musical instruments
___ Can remember songs

INTRAPERSONAL

___ Likes to be alone
___ Is reflective
___ Doesn't give in to peer pressure
___ Likes to ponder and ask questions
___ Can be shy
___ Has a strong sense of right and wrong
___ Is interested in personal goals
___ Can readily identify own strengths and weaknesses

LOGICAL/ MATHEMATICAL

___ Likes math
___ Enjoys logic puzzles
___ Likes computers
___ Is organized
___ Can think critically
___ Likes to analyze things
___ Is good at mental math
___ Likes strategy games
___ Likes clearly defined answers

BODILY/KINESTHETIC

___ Is good at sports
___ Prefers to do things and not just watch
___ Uses hands when speaking
___ Likes working with hands
___ Is well coordinated
___ Gets restless if sits too long
___ Catches on quickly to physical skills
___ Looks forward to P.E.

INTERPERSONAL

___ Likes working with a group
___ Likes to be the center of attention
___ Has many friends
___ Likes to organize
___ Has good leadership skills
___ Is a good motivator
___ Wins confidence of others
___ Is sensitive to others' feelings

NATURALIST

___ Likes to be outdoors
___ Collects natural objects, such as rocks
___ Likes to classify things
___ Often knows names of plants/animals
___ Is flexible
___ Enjoys crafts involving nature
___ Has keen sense of nature exploration
___ Likes outdoor recreation, such as camping

Reproducible

Student Learning Contract

NAME:_____

I am interested in learning about _____

_____.

Here is exactly what I plan to learn: _____

_____.

I will use the following resources: _____

_____.

My finished product will be _____

_____

_____

_____.

It will be finished on _____.

I will present my product on _____.

STUDENT SIGNATURE: _____

TEACHER SIGNATURE: _____

DATE: _____

eproducible

Signal Cards

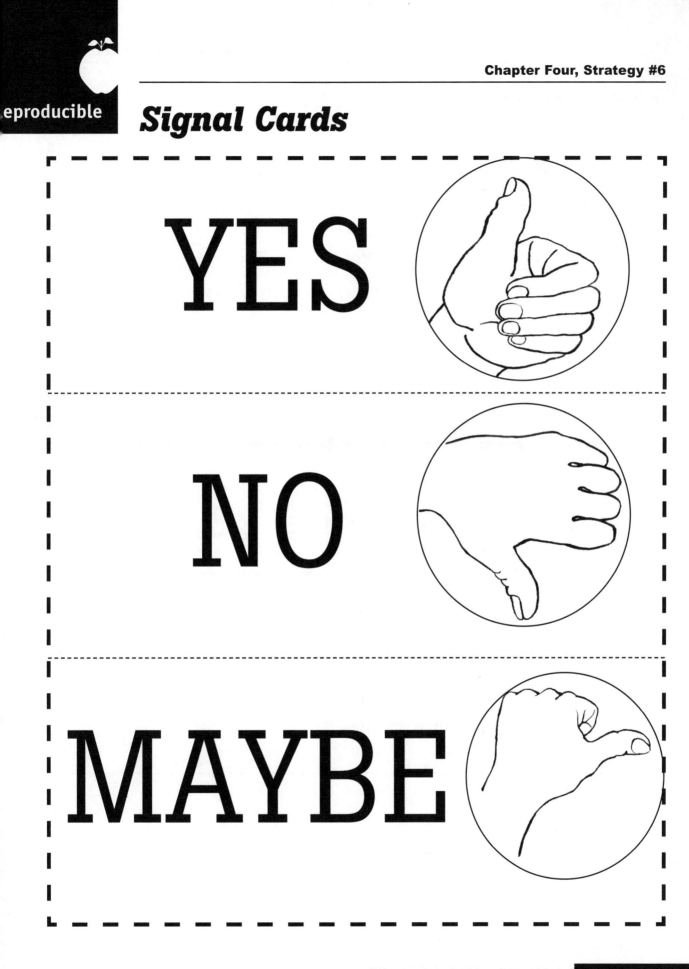

Reproducible

How Am I Doing?

Name of student: _____

Date: _____

The mark on the continuum below represents how well I succeeded in meeting my learning goals today.

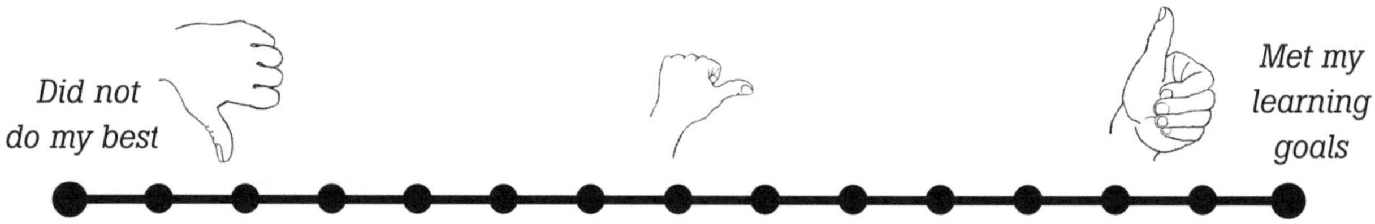

Did not do my best ●—●—●—●—●—●—●—●—●—●—●—●—●—●—● *Met my learning goals*

Here is what I accomplished: _____

_____

_____

_____

Here is my plan for tomorrow. _____

_____

_____

_____

Reproducible

Four Square Products

VISUAL
Advertisement
Collage
Poster
Flowchart
Venn diagram
Painting
Map
Video
Story map
Timeline
T chart

AUDITORY
Audiotape
News broadcast
Speech
Debate
Lecture
Group discussion
Interview
Round table discussion
Book review
Teach others

KINESTHETIC
A model
Performance of a dance
or skit
Sculpture
Mobile
Diorama
Dramatization
Experiment
Pantomime
Role play
Display

WRITTEN
Book report
Letter
Poetry
Research paper
Story
Checklist
Journal
Essay
Newsletter
Survey

Reproducible

Kinesthetic Assessment

Reproducible

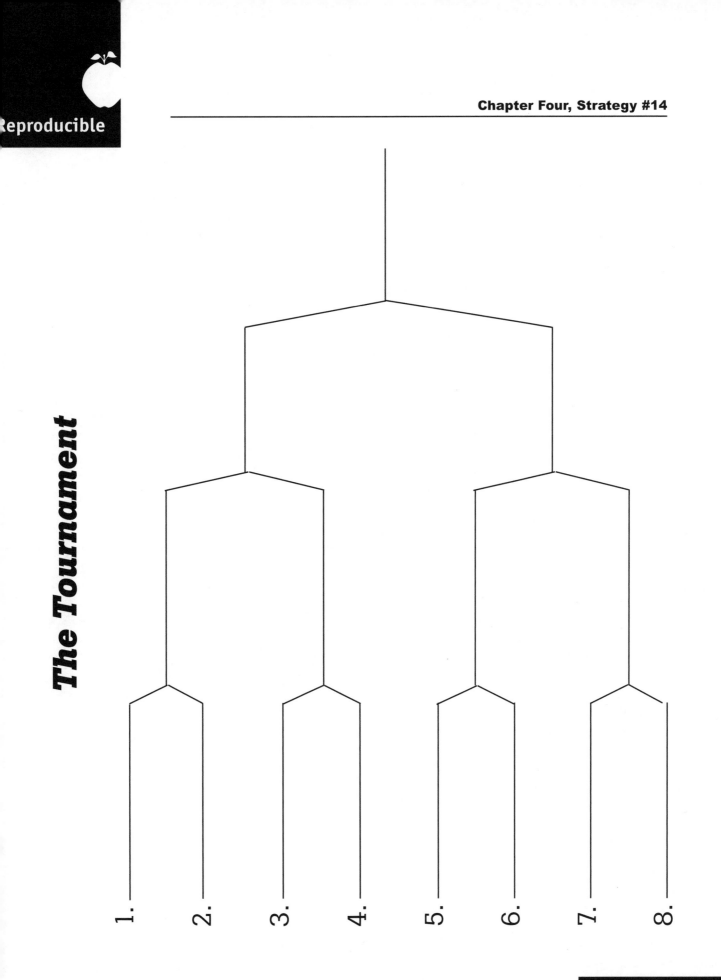

The Tournament

1.

2.

3.

4.

5.

6.

7.

8.

Recommended Resources

Print Resources

Allen, Janet. *Tools for Teaching Content Literacy.* Portland, ME: Stenhouse Publishers, 2004.

Aronson, E., N. Blaney, C. Stephin, J. Sikes, and M. Snapp. *The Jigsaw Classroom.* Beverly Hills, CA: Sage Publishing Co., 1978.

Beers, Kyleen. *When Kids Can't Read: What Teachers Can Do.* Portsmouth, NH: Heinemann, 2002.

Buehl, Doug. *Classroom Strategies for Interactive Learning.* Newark, DE: International Reading Association, 2001.

Burke, Jim. *The English Teacher's Companion: A Complete Guide to Classroom, Curriculum, and the Profession.* Portsmouth, NH: Heinemann, 2003.

Forsten, Char, Jim Grant, and Betty Hollas. *Differentiated Instruction: Different Strategies for Different Learners.* Peterborough, NH: Crystal Springs Books, 2002.

———. *Differentiating Textbooks: Strategies to Improve Student Comprehension and Motivation.* Peterborough, NH: Crystal Springs Books, 2003.

Gregory, Gayle H., and Carolyn Chapman. *Differentiated Instructional Strategies: One Size Doesn't Fit All.* Thousand Oaks, CA: Corwin Press, 2001.

Heacox, Diane. *Differentiating Instruction in the Regular Classroom: How to Reach and Teach All Learners, Grades 3–12.* Minneapolis, MN: Free Spirit Publishing, Inc., 2002.

Jensen, Eric. *Brain-Compatible Strategies.* San Diego, CA: The Brain Store, 1997.

———. *Teaching with the Brain in Mind.* Alexandria, VA: Association for Supervision and Curriculum Development, 1998.

Johnson, Nancy L. *Active Questioning: Questioning Still Makes the Difference.* Marion, IL: Pieces of Learning, 1996.

———. *Questioning Makes the Difference.* Marion, IL: Pieces of Learning, 1990.

Kagan, Spencer. *Cooperative Learning.* San Clemente, CA: Kagan Publishing and Professional Development, 1994.

———. *Thinking Questions Smart Card.* San Clemente, CA: Kagan Publishing and Professional Development, 1999.

———, and Miguel Kagan. *Multiple Intelligences: The Complete MI Book.* San Clemente, CA: Kagan Publishing and Professional Development, 1998.

Kingore, Bertie. *Differentiation: Simplified, Realistic, and Effective.* Austin, TX: Professional Associates Publishing, 2004.

Marzano, Robert J., Jennifer S. Norford, Diane E. Paynter, Debra J. Pickering, and Barbara B. Gaddy. *A Handbook for Classroom Instruction that Works.* New York, NY: Prentice Hall, 2004.

Pike, Robert W. *Creative Training Techniques Handbook: Tips, Tactics, and How-Tos for Delivering Effective Training.* Minneapolis, MN: Lakewood Books, 1989.

Raphael, Taffy A., Kathy Highfield, and Kathryn H. Au. *QAR Now: A Powerful and Practical Framework That Develops Comprehension and Higher-Level Thinking in All Students.* New York, NY: Scholastic, 2006.

Slavin, Robert E. *Cooperative Learning: Theory, Research, and Practice (2nd Edition)*. Boston, MA: Allyn & Bacon, 1994.

Sousa, David. *How the Gifted Brain Learns*. Thousand Oaks, CA: Corwin Press, 2002.

———. *How the Special Needs Brain Learns*. Thousand Oaks, CA: Corwin Press, 2001.

Tomlinson, Carol Ann. *The Differentiated Classroom: Responding to the Needs of All Learners*. Alexandria, VA: Association for Supervision and Curriculum Development, 1999.

———, and Susan Demirsky Allan. *How to Differentiate Instruction in Mixed-Ability Classrooms*. Alexandria, VA: Association for Supervision and Curriculum Development, 2001.

Von Oech, Roger. *A Kick in the Seat of the Pants: Using Your Explorer, Artist, Judge, and Warrior To Be More Creative*. New York, NY: Harper & Row Publishers, Inc., 1986.

———. *A Whack on the Side of the Head: How to Unlock Your Mind for Innovation*. New York, NY: Warner Books, 1983.

Web Sites

www.crystalsprings.com
for books and other products to support differentiated instruction

www.help4teachers.com
for samples of differentiated lessons

www.kaganonline.com
for cooperative learning materials

www.sde.com
for training and other support in implementing differentiated instruction

www.teachingmadeeasier.com
for hundreds of ways to work smarter when creating materials for the classroom

Index

A

Accountability, individual and group
  building, 63–64, 68, 69, 70
  evaluating, 64, *130*
  norms for, 64, *131*
Anchor activities, with flexible grouping, 65, 76, 78
Anticipation Guide, 89
Anything-but-Horizontal Reading-Tac-Toe
  for Expository Text, *141*
  for Short Fiction, *140*
Appointment Calendar, 17–18, *102*
Assessment, ongoing, 12, 13. *See also* Formative
      assessment; Pre-assessment;
      Summative assessment
  beginning, 82, *144–46*
  definition of, 82
  in differentiated instruction, 83
  flexible grouping activities for, 67, 69, *133*
  reflection and action planning for, 99
  strategies for
    Anticipation Guide, 89
    Exit Cards, 91
    Five-Finger Reading Gauge, 86
    Four Square Products, 95, *149*
    Handshake or High Five, 87
    Human Continuum, 85
    Kinesthetic Assessment, 96, *150*
    Learning Logs & Response Journals, 94
    Signal Cards, 90, *147*
    Student Self-Assessment, 92, *148*
    Synectics, 97
    Three Facts & a Fib, 93
    Tournament, The, 98, *151*
    Word Toss, 88
  student-engagement activities for, 24, 25
  using data from, 83–84
Auditory learners
  questioning activities for, 44–45, 46–47, *108,*
      117
  student-engagement activities for, 15, 21

Author-and-Me questions, 49, 50, 51, *119, 122*

B

Ballas, George, 34
Bloom, Benjamin, 35
Bloom's Cube, 44, *111*
Bloom's Taxonomy, 35
  in cubing strategy, 44–45, *111–13*
  Key Words & Sample Questions from, 40, 52,
      105–6
  in questioning activity, 48
Blue Role Cards for Expository Text, 73, *136*
Boredom in learning, sources of, 14
Brainstorming activities, 67, 70, *133*
Brainstorming A–Z, 67, *133*
Button pushers, dealing with, 24

C

Calendar, Appointment, 17–18, *102*
Carousel Your Way Through a K–W–L, 20–21
Categorization, student-engagement activity for,
      28–29
Change, difficulty of, 100
Choices, in demonstrating learning, 84
Circle the Category, 28–29
Comparisons, Synectics for, 97
Comprehension Cube, 45, *113*
Concept Map, for exploring fairness, 66, *132*
Content review
  in brainstorming activities, 67, 70, *133*
  student-engagement activities for, 24–25, 30
Contract, Student Learning, 82, *146*
Cooperative learning structure, with flexible
      grouping activities, 68–69, 70
Critical thinking, questioning activity for, 54–55,
      128
Cube Pattern, *110*
Cubing, as questioning activity, 41–45, *107–13*
Cubing & Bloom's, 44–45, *111–13*
Curriculum accessibility, strategies for, 18

Note: Page numbers in *italics* indicate reproducibles.

D

D.E.A.Q. (Drop Everything And Question), 52, *105–6*

Differentiated instruction
benefits of, 13
challenges of, 11–13
meaning of, 13
reflection and action planning for, 31–32, 59, 80, 99
starting, 100
as student centered, 34

Differentiated Wait Time, 38–39

Differentiation, questions as form of, 35

Directions
how to give, 25, 86
modeling, 55

Discussion, flexible grouping for, 71–75, *135–38*

Discussion Cards for Narrative Text, 74–75, *138*

Discussion Roles for a Lecture or Video, 71–72, *134*

E

Engagement, student. *See* Student engagement

Evaluation, as part of assessment, 82

Exit Cards, 91

Expository Text
Anything-but-Horizontal Reading-Tac-Toe for, *141*
Role Cards for, 73, *135–37*

F

Fair & Equal Are Not the Same, 66, *132*

Fairness, exploring, 66

Five-Finger Reading Gauge, 86

Five in a group, in flexible grouping, 63

Five Questions to Ask, 58, *129*

Fixed grouping, 60

Flexible grouping, 12, 13
accountability in, 63–64, 68, 69, 70, *130–31*
"Ask Three Before Me" rule for, 60
description of, 60–61
in differentiated instruction, 65
vs. fixed grouping, 60
group size in, 63
guidelines for, 62–63
names for, 62
reflection and action planning for, 80
sample roles in, 63

Flexible grouping (*continued*)
strategies for
Brainstorming A–Z, 67, *133*
Discussion Cards for Narrative Text, 74–75, *138*
Discussion Roles for a Lecture or Video, 71–72, *134*
Fair & Equal Are Not the Same, 66, *132*
4–6–8, 77, *143*
Jigsaw, 68–69
Numbered Heads Together, 63, 70
R.A.F.T. (Role, Audience, Format, Topic), 78–79
Role Cards for Expository Text, 73, *135–37*
Think-Tac-Toe, 76, *139–42*
teacher as coach and facilitator for, 64–65
types of, 61–62

Foreign languages, name-tag activity for, 27

Formative assessment, 83, 84
strategies for, 90–92, *147, 148*

4–6–8, activity, 77, *143*

Four Square Products, 95, *149*

F.R.E.D. (Facts, Reflections, Evaluation, and Decisions), for encouraging critical thinking, 54–55, *128*

G

Geometric Questions, Parking Lot &, 37, *103–4*

Getting-acquainted activity, 23

Grading, as part of assessment, 82

Green Role Cards for Expository Text, 73, *137*

Group leaders, selecting, 83

Group Norms, 64, *131*

Groups. *See also* Flexible grouping
managing formation of, 28
types of, 61–62

H

Handshake or High Five, 87

Heterogeneous groups, uses for, 61–62, 71

Higher-level thinking, questions stimulating, 35–36, 40, 44, 53

High Five, Handshake or, 87

"Hogs" vs. "logs"
cooperative learning structure for, 70
paraphrasing activity for, 19

Note: Page numbers in *italics* indicate reproducibles.

Homogeneous groups, uses for, 62, 73, 74

How Am I Doing?, 92, *148*

How Well Did We Work Together?, 64, *130*

Human Continuum, 85

I

I Do Have a Question, 40, *105–6*

I Have/Who Has?, 46–47, *114*

Independent or individual work, uses for, 62

Independent projects, for students who know the topic, 21

Informal Rating Scale to Discover Intelligences, 82, *145*

In-My-Head questions, 49–50, *119, 122–23*

Intelligences, identifying, 82, *144–45*

Interests, Intelligences & Ignorances Survey, 82, *144*

Internet
  learning-styles test on, 43
  Web sites on, 155

In-the-Book questions, 49, *119, 120–21*

J

Jigsaw, 68–69

Journal prompts, for exploring fairness, 66

K

Key Words & Sample Questions from Bloom's Taxonomy, 40, 52, *105–6*

Kinesthetic Assessment, 96, *150*

Kinesthetic learners
  questioning activities for, 44–45, *109, 118*
  student-engagement activities for, 15, 18, 21, 22

K–W–L strategy, carousel activity for, 20–21

L

Learning Logs & Response Journals, 94

Learning-styles test, on Internet, 43

Lecture, Discussion Roles for, 71–72, *134*

Listening
  active, in brainstorming activity, 67, *133*
  strategy improving, 46–47

List making, in brainstorming activity, 67, *133*

Literacy, D.E.A.Q. strategy for, 52

Literature
  for exploring fairness, 66
  response journals on, 94

"Logs" vs. "hogs"
  cooperative learning structure for, 70
  paraphrasing activity for, 19

M

Math
  D.E.A.Q. activity for, 52
  name-tag activity for, 27

Math Cube, 45, *112*

Milling to Music, 30

Modeling directions, 55

Movement into groups, managing, 28

Music activity, for reviewing content, 30

N

Name-tag activity, for reinforcing learning, 27

Narrative Text, Discussion Cards for, 74–75, *138*

Numbered Heads Together, 63, 70

Nutrition unit, Think-Tac-Toe for, 76

O

On-My-Own questions, 49, 50, 51, *119, 123*

Organizers, graphic
  for questions while reading, 58, *129*
  Tournament, 98, *151*

P

Pairs, in flexible grouping, 63

Paraphrase, Timed-Pair, 19

Parking Lot & Geometric Questions, 37, *103–4*

Planning Questions Are the Key, 56–57

Pointer/Signal Words, 73, *135*

Portfolios, for student self-assessment, 92

Pre-assessment, 82, 83, *144–46*
  strategies for, 85–89

Predicting
  pre-assessment activity for, 88
  student-engagement activity for, 24–25

Project designs, for exploring fairness, 66

Q

Q.A.R. strategy, for answering questions, 49–51, *119–23*

Quads, in flexible grouping, 63

Note: Page numbers in *italics* indicate reproducibles.

Question-Answer Relationships (Q.A.R.), 49–51, *119–23*

Questioning, 12, 13

    benefits of, 34

    de-emphasis of, 33–34

    in differentiated instruction, 36

    with higher-level questions, 35–36

    importance of, as student-centered activity, 33, 34, 35, 36

    reflection and action planning for, 59

    Signal Cards used with, 90, *147*

    strategies for, 48, *115–18*

        Cubing & Bloom's, 44–45, *111–13*

        D.E.A.Q. (Drop Everything And Question), 52, *105–6*

        Differentiated Wait Time, 38–39

        Five Questions to Ask, 58, *129*

        I Do Have a Question, 40, *105–6*

        I Have/Who Has?, 46–47, *114*

        Parking Lot & Geometric Questions, 37, *103–4*

        Planning Questions Are the Key, 56–57

        Question-Answer Relationships, 49–51, *119–23*

        Question Stems & Cubing, 41–43, *107–10*

        Question-Tac-Toe, 48, *115–18*

        Talk with F.R.E.D., 54–55, *128*

        T.H.I.N.K., 53, *124–27*

    by teacher, 33, 35–36

    time restraints on, 33

Question Stems & Cubing, 41–43, *107–10*

Question-Tac-Toe, 48, *115–18*

R

R.A.F.T. (Role, Audience, Format, Topic), 78–79

Reading

    flexible grouping activities for, 73–77, *135–43*

    pre-assessment activities for, 86, 88–89

    questioning activity for, 58, *129*

    student-engagement activity for, 28–29

Reproducibles

    Anything-but-Horizontal Reading-Tac-Toe

        for Expository Text, *141*

        for Short Fiction, *140*

    Appointment Calendar, *102*

    Blue Role Cards for Expository Text, *136*

    Brainstorming A–Z, *133*

Reproducibles *(continued)*

    Concept Map, *132*

    cubing

        for Auditory Learners, *108*

        Bloom's Cube, *111*

        Comprehension Cube, *113*

        Cube Pattern, *110*

        for Kinesthetic Learners, *109*

        Math Cube, *112*

        for Visual Learners, *107*

    Discussion Cards for Narrative Text, *138*

    Five Questions to Ask, *129*

    4–6–8, *143*

    Four Square Products, *149*

    Green Role Cards for Expository Text, *137*

    Group Norms, *131*

    How Am I Doing?, *148*

    How Well Did We Work Together?, *130*

    I Have/Who Has?, *114*

    Interests, Intelligences & Ignorances Survey, *144*

    Key Words & Sample Questions from Bloom's Taxonomy, *105–6*

    Kinesthetic Assessment, *150*

    118 T.H.I.N.K. Questions, *124–27*

    Parking Lot & Geometric Questions, *103–4*

    Pointer/Signal Words, *135*

    Question-Answer Relationships (Q.A.R.), *119*

        Level I Questions, *120*

        Level II Questions, *121*

        Level III Questions, *122*

        Level IV Questions, *123*

    Question-Tac-Toe, *115*

        for Auditory Learners, *117*

        for Kinesthetic Learners, *118*

        for Visual Learners, *116*

    Role Cards for a Lecture or Video, *134*

    Signal Cards, *147*

    Student Learning Contract, *146*

    Talk with F.R.E.D., *128*

    Think-Tac-Toe, *139*

    Think-Tac-Toe the MI Way, *142*

    Tournament, The, *151*

Response Journals, Learning Logs &, 94

Review, content

    in brainstorming activities, 67, 70, *133*

    student-engagement activities for, 24–25, 30

Note: Page numbers in *italics* indicate reproducibles.

Right-There questions, 49, 50, 51, *119, 120*
Role Cards for a Lecture or Video, 71–72, *134*
Role Cards for Expository Text, 73, *135–37*
Rubrics, for assessment, 92, 95
Rules, classroom, establishing, 97

S

Science
    creating differentiated assignments in, 57
    D.E.A.Q. strategy for, 52
    name-tag activity for, 27
Self-Assessment, Student, 92, *148*
Shared responsibility for learning, 55, 69
Short Fiction, Anything-but-Horizontal Reading-
        Tac-Toe for, *140*
Show—Don't Tell, 22
Signal Cards, 90, *147*
Small groups
    of like readiness, uses for, 62
    of varying degrees of readiness, uses for,
        61–62
Snowball Fight, 24–25
Social studies
    D.E.A.Q. strategy for, 52
    Jigsaw strategy for, 68, 69
Struggling writers, 94
Student-centered instruction, importance of, 34–35
Student engagement, 12, 13
    in differentiated instruction, 14–15
    reflection and action planning for, 31–32
    strategies for
        Appointment Calendar, 17–18, *102*
        Carousel Your Way Through a K–W–L,
            20–21
        Circle the Category, 28–29
        emphasis of, 16
        Milling to Music, 30
        Show—Don't Tell, 22
        Snowball Fight, 24–25
        That's Me!, 23
        Timed-Pair Paraphrase, 19
        Vote with Your Feet & Not Your Hands, 26
        What's My Name?, 27
    teaching styles and, 15–16
Student Learning Contract, 82, *146*
Student Self-Assessment, 92, *148*

Summarizing, student-engagement activity for,
        24–25
Summative assessment, 83
    strategies for, 93–98, *149–51*
Synectics, 97

T

Talk with F.R.E.D., 54–55, *128*
Teaching styles
    adjusting, for differentiated instruction, 16
    types of, 15–16
TeachTimers, 28
That's Me!, 23
Think, Search, and Find questions, 49, 50, 51, *119,
        121*
T.H.I.N.K., 53, *124–27*
Think-Tac-Toe, 76, *139–42*
Think-Tac-Toe the MI Way, *142*
Three Facts & a Fib, 93
Timed-Pair Paraphrase, 19
Tournament, The, 98, *151*
Triads, in flexible grouping, 63

V

Video, Discussion Roles for, 71–72, *134*
Videotaping, for analyzing questioning, 36
Visual learners
    questioning activities for, 44–45, *107, 116*
    student-engagement activities for, 15, 21, 22
Vocabulary building
    assessment activity for, 96, *150*
    student-engagement activities for, 22, 28–29
Vote with Your Feet & Not Your Hands, 26

W

Wait time, differentiated
    questioning activities for, 37–39, *103–4*
    students in need of, 39
Web sites, 155
What's My Name?, 27
Whole-class instruction, vs. flexible grouping, 60
Whole group, uses for, 61
Word Toss, 88
Writing
    assessment activities for, 91, 94
    flexible grouping activity for, 78–79

Note: Page numbers in *italics* indicate reproducibles.